Pure Passion

MARION DUCKWORTH

VICTOR BOOKS

A DIVISION OF SCRIPTURE PRESS PUBLICATIONS INC.
USA CANADA ENGLAND

Editor: Carolyn Nystrom
Cover Design: Grace K. Chan Mallette
Cover Photo: William Koechling

Library of Congress Cataloging-in-Publication Date

Duckworth, Marion.
    Pure passion / Marion Duckworth.
       p. cm. — (The Tapestry collection)
    ISBN 1-56476-222-X
    1. Sex—Biblical teaching. 2. Bible. O.T. Song of Solomon—Devotional literature. I. Title. II. Series.
BS680.S5D83 1994   93-45044
223'.906—dc20   CIP

1 2 3 4 5 6 7 8 9 10 Printing/Year 98 97 96 95 94

CONTENTS

Introduction   5

1   SING A SONG OF SOLOMON   7
    Overview of the Poem: Part 1

2   CELEBRATE MARITAL INTIMACY   16
    Overview of the Poem: Part 2

3   COURTSHIP AND ROMANCE   25
    Song of Solomon 1:1-17

4   WHEN PASSION IS PURE   35
    Song of Solomon 2:1-17

5   THE LANGUAGE OF LOVE   46
    Song of Solomon 3:1–5:1

6   NEW PASSION FOR OLD MARRIAGES   57
    Song of Solomon 5:2–6:3

7   LOVING FOR LIFE   69
    Song of Solomon 6:4–8:14

8   THE SONG AS ALLEGORY   81
    Overview: Part 3

Just You and You: Group Study Guide   93

Endnotes   109

31167

INTRODUCTION

"I remember when I was eighteen and came across the Song of Solomon," said Annie. "Wow!"

My friend Annie and I were talking about my current writing project: a Bible study book on Solomon's poem. I laughed at Annie's reminiscence, because I remembered how the book had affected me when I first read it. It was the same feeling when, as a schoolgirl, I had discovered photographs of naked natives in *National Geographic.*

All through the writing of this book, I've been as excited as when I finally lost those last five pounds and reached my weight goal. That's because I've become convinced that the Song of Solomon communicates a message about sex that women are aching to hear.

Song of Solomon speaks of the purity of marital love play and coitus. The poem is sensual. It uses words like *breast* in a sexual context. It plays with metaphors for intercourse. The book strikes a blow at our stodgy presuppositions, and I believe God means it to do just that.

🐝 *Just You and God.* Because of the private nature of this subject, it is entirely appropriate to begin your study alone. With God. So each of the eight chapters opens with a section of personal study. Since this book is designed for women with busy lives, five-day segments mark division points in each chapter. So, for example, you'll read the brief introductory narrative for *Monday*, then write the answers to the five questions for that day. Then the next day you follow a similar outline for *Tuesday.* If you prefer, of course, you can spend more than one day on the questions. Questions are designed to help you think through a passage of Scripture and arrive at it's main truths *for yourself*—a skill that is essential in order to use the Bible as a guide for life. Personal study tools include an English dictionary and two or three translations of the Bible—including one in modern English. Each day of study includes questions to help you integrate biblical truths with your personal experience. These questions of application often have multiple answers that will differ from person to person.

🍎 *Just You and Me* appears at the close of each chapter. This section is designed for use with your husband. Choose at least one activity there to complete together.

🍎 *Just You and You* is a group study guide appearing in the back of the book. It outlines an hour's worth of discussion questions and activities for women who want to interact with each other about their personal responses to this fascinating book of Scripture.

Approach Song of Solomon reflectively, looking into the deep places of your soul. Ask yourself:

—How do my attitudes toward sexual expression in my marriage need to change?
—What steps do I need to take to begin the process?

Begin each day's study prayerfully, expecting God to whisper insight into the most private areas of your life.

One final note about the reality of the stories in this book. The stories are true—real events, real feelings, real people—generously shared by those who told them. But to protect privacy, I have changed each name. I'm sure the reader will understand.

SING A SONG OF SOLOMON
Overview: Part 1

JUST YOU AND GOD

In his romantic love poem, King Solomon memorializes the passionate relationship between himself and his beloved. If you've never read this book, you may be surprised by its vivid, explicit language, but the language is typical of the way poets of the ninth century B.C. wrote.

What a far cry is this description of marital love and sex from the Victorian silence that surrounded the subject earlier in our century. Then, the word *intercourse* wasn't spoken from the pulpit or in dignified parlors. Sexual passion seemed unchristian, perhaps even dirty, or at least tainted by the fall.

Today we live in a time of backlash in which intercourse has been reduced to an "act," passion to animalism, and love-making to "lust-making." Solomon, in his poem (also called *Canticles*, and thought by some to be a collection of poems), sweeps away the extremes. In a sensual style, he paints with pure brush-strokes a stunning picture of marital love that is meant to firmly set our passion in the place God intended.

Monday
I know something of the elation David and Bathsheba must have felt when God gifted them with Solomon after they had lost a one-week-old child. That's because, like them, I saw a cherished baby buried after one week of life. In my case, the child who died was my granddaughter, Katherine, taken because of a birth defect. The gift that came later was twin grandsons.

Solomon was treasured by his parents because he was the oldest living son of their relationship. It was Solomon to whom David promised the throne of Israel. When David was old and ill, he anointed Solomon king.

Father had wanted to build a temple for God. But God said no. Son was chosen instead to execute his father's wishes. The building of that temple of stone and cedar, gold and olivewood, took seven years. Upon its completion, priests brought the ark of the covenant into the most holy place. Then the glory of the Lord filled the temple so completely that the priests couldn't perform their service.

Had David lived to see it, I'm sure he would have felt enormously pleased with his beloved son's accomplishment — the construction of the most important building in all of Israel, the temple in which Jehovah Himself would dwell. David would have been proud too, because Solomon completed the assignment with great honor. He did so for himself, for his father, and for Jehovah.

In one sitting read through the Song of Solomon. (It takes about fifteen minutes.) Be sure to use a Bible version that tells which main character is speaking. Since Solomon's Song is a poem written to express an *experience*, read from your heart. Don't worry if the ancient poetic style is unfamiliar. Right now, try to *become* the original characters by putting yourself in the place of each so that the story will be more real to you. Answer the following questions as you read.

1. What names do two different versions of the Bible give to the three main characters: the woman, the man, and the friends?

2. As you imagine yourself to be these characters, write your thoughts and feelings.

3. What colors would you choose to paint the sex scenes in this book? Why? What colors would you choose to illustrate today's view of sex as seen on television and in films? Why?

4. Not many men today would write a poem like this to their wives. How do you think today's man would likely express similar feelings?

5. Write a paragraph describing your strongest reactions when you read through the Song of Solomon. Explain in your paragraph why you feel that way.

Make Proverbs 18:15 the basis of a prayer in which you ask to know the truth from Scripture about married love. Ask God to be your teacher.

Tuesday

Why is poetry included in the Bible? Poems can teach, but their main function is to enrich our devotional lives.

One timeless purpose of Solomon's poem is to celebrate our sexuality as God-given. Grasp the lilting tone of the man and woman as they sing of their physical love. Think of that the next time a sweaty bedroom scene flashes on television or you see an advertisement for the newest literary sleaze.

J. Vernon McGee writes, "This book . . . will be abused by carnal Christians. But if you are one who is walking with the Lord, if the Lord Jesus means a great deal to you and you love Him, then this little book will mean a great deal to you."[1]

1. Popular song lyrics are modern poetry. Sum up the message that one popular song gives about sex.

2. Poetry is sprinkled throughout Scripture, but Job, Psalms, and Ecclesiastes are composed entirely of poems. Look through these three books and find a passage in each where the authors wrote of deep feelings the way Solomon did in the Song. Make notes about the special meaning each has for you.

3. Psalmists' poems or song lyrics often describe struggles and journeys upward. These lyrics become spikes driven into the rock-face of our own spiritual climb. Choose a psalm that appeals to you for that reason. Journal to God about a specific way this psalm helps you.

4. Poets express themselves in a language of pictures. What everyday experiences do you think the following phrases pictured? What words might you use to picture a similar experience in today's language?

Passage	Experience in Solomon's day	What you might use today
"Like a mare" 1:9 "Like a flock of goats" 4:1 "Like sheep just shorn" 4:2 "Your plants are an orchard of pomegranates" 4:13		

5. A poet also uses repetition for emphasis. Read the following passages and find words or their derivations repeated within each verse. Decide what point Solomon is making through each repetition.

🐛 1:3a

🐛 1:5

🐛 1:6

🕊 3:1

🕊 6:1

Wednesday
As a hero, Solomon, the third king of Israel and the person named "Lover" in this poem, seems to have no counterpart in modern western civilization. He wasn't just another handsome face; he seemed to have *everything*.

But Bible writers, unlike some who write biographies in ordinary literature, don't portray their main characters in one dimension — highlighting only their winsomeness, but ignoring their foibles and faults. In these pages, writers *tell it all*.

We learn, for example, that Solomon accumulated an enormous harem. Many women were gifts from foreign leaders, and their presence became a temptation that the King wasn't strong enough to overcome.

So with all those women at his disposal, how could Solomon have had such a loving relationship with the *one* about whom he wrote in his Song? Perhaps because this particular relationship was not a marriage of convenience. It was a union made by choice out of love.

1. What piece of writing appeals to you as a modern love story? What do you like most about it? Does the hero seem human or too perfect?

2. Solomon is described in other Scriptures besides the Song. Read 1 Kings 4:29-34 and note how this account contributes to your picture of him. How many songs did Solomon write? How is the Song of Solomon distinguished among them? (See Song 1:1.)

3. In a society where polygamy was common, why do you think God gave the command about it in Deuteronomy 17:14-17?

4. Read 1 Kings 11:1-6. What is the tone of God's assessment of Solomon in later years? In view of God's commands about polygamy, why do you think God allowed Solomon's love poem to become part of Scripture?

5. According to 1 Kings 11:4-6, what was the process of decline in Solomon's moral life? What do you learn from the King's experience? Reflect on 1 Kings 11:4 and ask God to sensitize you to that kind of sin.

Thursday
If tabloid journalism existed in Solomon's day and paparazzi dogged the couples' steps the way they do modern royalty, what photos do you suppose we'd see? Solomon with hay fever, his eyes and nose red and swollen? The Shulammite, tight-lipped, sullen, and bloated with PMS?

No doubt, there would have been such photo opportunities simply because even kings and queens have good and bad days. None of us — royalty or commoner — always looks and feels our best. But in his poem, Solomon writes more about bliss than blahs.

Like Solomon and his bride, we and our husbands are typical combinations of strengths and weaknesses. As a result, no marital union is one long romantic interlude. Have you expected your mate to reflect an ideal that doesn't exist?

1. Look back at a romantically blissful time that you and your husband enjoyed. Recapture your feelings. Record the reasons for why it is a treasured memory. Write a sentence thanking God for special times like this.

2. Scan the poem. List five positive attributes that Beloved describes in the poem about Lover?

3. What five positive qualities would you include in a character sketch of your mate?

4. Read Song of Solomon 1:6, 8, 15; 6:4-9. Write a brief description of the woman in Solomon's Song. Include the way she looked, the work she did, where she was from, and members of her immediate family.

5. Based on the Beloved's attitude toward her husband, what Valentine message do you think she might write to him?

Friday
Imagine the title on a theater marquee, in TV Guide, or in the video store: *Song of Solomon, the Movie.* Not too far-fetched, for this poem has all the romance, drama, and tension necessary. In the first section, "The Beginning of Love," chapters 1–4, a peasant girl becomes the bride of a wealthy and powerful king.[2] Part of the drama unfolds in a palace breathtaking with its sumptuousness.

In the second section, "The Broadening of Love," chapters 5–8, conflict enters.[3] Beloved is unresponsive to Lover, and his absence plays a significant role. But the two resolve their problems and unite once again in one another's arms. They go on to describe the nature of true love and vow commitment to one another.

1. Pretend that you are a film student assigned to make a movie based on the Song of Solomon. Write a note to your professor listing reservations you may have.

2. Whom would you cast as hero and heroine?

3. Why would you feel comfortable calling the book on which the movie is based *inspired by* God even though God's name isn't mentioned in it? (See John 5:39.)

4. Assume that you are a stage manager planning a scene based on Song 3:6-11. Jot down ways you'd make it memorable. Or make sketches of your ideas.

5. If you think a film based on this book would be too graphic, is it because society with its degenerated attitudes would misinterpret it, or is it too graphic because of the nature of the poem itself?

   If you feel that such a film could be helpful, what kind of help might it provide?

   Reflect before God about ways your attitude toward sex is being affected by society and write down what He shows you.

6. Begin a letter to your husband on subjects covered in this chapter. At the end of each chapter, you'll add another paragraph. The purpose of this letter is to talk to him on paper about discoveries you've made.

Issues from this chapter you could address in your letter include:
- Your impression of this explicit, sexual love poem and your strongest reactions.
- Reasons why you think Solomon is an important figure in the Bible—his strengths and weaknesses—and what these have shown you.
- Times of your own romance that this poem reminds you of.
- Your ideas for making a movie about the Song of Solomon.

JUST YOU AND ME: For Husbands and Wives

- If you were collaborating on a script based on your own marriage, what new scenes would you like to be able to include that haven't yet taken place in your real lives?

- Recall a love song that has had particular meaning to you. Remind your husband of it and see how many of the lyrics you can remember. Decide whether you still consider it "Our Song."

- Go through photograph albums or keepsakes that depict times the two of you spent together. Take turns telling the other, "When I think of this, I. . . ."

- If your husband is unfamiliar with the Song of Solomon, tell him why you think that it's an exciting book. Read aloud to him a section that you particularly like. Ask what he thinks about having a book like this in the Bible.

- If your husband is familiar with the poem, ask him to select one of Lover's speeches to read to you. Then read one of Beloved's speeches to him. Talk about how that makes each of you feel.

CELEBRATE MARITAL INTIMACY
Overview: Part 2

JUST YOU AND GOD

"Was it good for you?" the muscular male lead in the TV miniseries whispers to the woman lying in bed next to him. They'd met earlier that evening in a cocktail lounge and later made their way up to his room.

She breathes a long, satisfied sigh. "Oh, yes. It was *so* good." They entwine, eyes closed.

As far as these characters are concerned, the evening was a success because they'd had good sex. This imaginary film clip typifies the most vocal amoral voices in society today: *Good sex—a pleasure we all deserve.*

Is it wrong to want good sex so long as it's not extramarital? Of course not. But good sex is more than learning to practice techniques that provide optimum pleasure. The foundation of truly *good* sex is to become convinced in our deepest of selves that sexual pleasure between man and wife is *good* in the biblical sense of the word.

That is where *good sex* begins.

Monday:
We know that Lover and Beloved are real people and not fictitious characters created in the mind of a novelist. But the fact that we meet them in an ancient poem may make them seem shadowy figures.

To help these people step out of the pages of divine literature and assume life, we'll look closely at the who, what, when, where, how, and why of scenes. To do that, we won't just study the Bible words or view the Song as an inspired description of two important historical figures. We'll get to know intimately these two flesh and blood people who existed in a particular place and at a particular time. We may even see ways that we, who live 3,000 years later, are like them.

By entering into their lives, instead of merely analyzing academically from the sidelines, we'll be better able to apply their principles of marital intimacy to our own unions. Get ready to have Lover and Beloved move into your life. Get ready to touch the fabric of their experiences, smell their fragrances, taste their delight, and see goodness at the core of it all.

1. In what kind of geographical setting did Beloved spend much of her time before marriage? (See Song 1:6.)

2. If you were doing the kind of work she did today, what kind of clothing would you wear? Keeping in mind that men and women wore tunics and belts made mostly from goat, sheep, or camel's hair, write a description of Beloved's costume for this scene in a film.

3. Look again at the information in Song 1:6-7. In a class-divided society, where do you think Beloved would fit?

4. According to Song 1:10-11 and 2:4a, what plans did Solomon have to change that?

5. Beloved's endearing name for Solomon is "Lover." What pet names do you have for your husband? Do your pet names communicate the same sentiment that hers do?

Which name do you think your husband likes best? Pray for God's leading as you settle on a flattering pet-name to use for your husband throughout this study.

Tuesday:
There's a big difference between things that are *private* and things that are *illicit*. What's private is personal, like the amount of your bank balance. Things that are illicit are improper.

Sexual intimacy between husband and wife is private and personal, but it is not illicit. We may have confused the two concepts, and what is *private* somehow seems wrong.

That sexuality is the naughty side of mankind is a devilish idea planted by Lucifer and carefully cultivated by his followers. Come to be called the "S" word, it has been wrapped in tawdriness and rated "X."

Pushing that mindset to the forefront is the secular media. "The only kind of sex that is forbidden on TV and in the movies is sex between husband and wife. . . . On TV, references to sex outside marriage are 14 times more common than sex inside marriage," complains Michael Medved.[1]

Not that the decline and fall of human sexuality is a modern phenomenon. The Canaanites who inhabited the Promised Land when the Israelites first came specialized in orgies. The Corinthians in the first century A.D. enlisted thousands of temple prostitutes as religious street-walkers.

In those heathen societies, illicit sex wore priestly garb. But it was not sex itself that was evil; only the way in which it was practiced. God calls women today to do now what he called our foremothers to do then: rip sex out of the hands of the Pretender and put it back in the place of purity and honor where it belongs.

1. Look up *good* in an English dictionary and list all the definitions that you think apply to *sex*.

2. Suppose that you are writing a book review of the Song of Solomon. Even though the statement "sex is good" doesn't appear in the book, what evidence would you give that the author sees sex that way?

3. What would you tell someone who insisted that sex was the original sin described in Genesis 3:1-7?

4. Sex is a God-given desire. Name as many other God-given desires as you can think of that can be used in either a right or a wrong way.

5. Underline key words in each of the two phrases from Genesis 1:31 that show marital intimacy as something pure that ought to be cherished: "God saw all that He had made, and it was very good." Journal your responses to God.

Wednesday:

Most of my life I saw my sexuality as organic. That is, I possessed certain organs that made me female and made sex possible. These organs allowed me to have intercourse and to procreate. Negative side effects were things like PMS and menstrual cramps.

But I had trouble identifying myself as sexual. Didn't sexuality have a negative connotation? What about single women? Were they sexual?

One author cleared up the matter for me. "We must distinguish between sexuality and sexual activity. My sexuality exists independently of what I do. It is a matter of identity, not behavior . . . to be human is to be sexual."[2]

The truth is this: while every woman may not have sex or bear children; every woman *is* sexual. She is the wondrous, glorious female of the species.

1. Read Song of Solomon 5:10-16. If the speaker's identity as female were not stated, and if that speaker did not use the personal pronoun, *his*, would you still know that the speaker was a woman speaking about a man? How?

2. If the speaker's identity as male were not stated in Song 4:1-5, how would you be able to tell that this was a man talking about a woman?

3. In what ways do the above speeches give you a fresh appreciation for the differences in the sexes?

   Are you pleased that you are female? Why or why not?

   After a shower or bath, stand in front of the mirror and, as nearly as you are able, appreciate your sexuality in a conversation with God.

4. From what you know about this poem, does the couple view sexual intimacy as only for procreation or for intimacy and enjoyment as well? Explain your answer.

5. Jot down references toward human sexuality that you hear and see this week on radio, TV, in print, and in conversation. Decide if each honors human sexuality or demeans it.

   If you were the member of a panel discussing the subject, what message would you like to communicate?

Thursday:

Few of us came into marriage without trailing wrong ideas about sex behind us. Here's how one woman describes her experiences:

> *When I was growing up, my parents never talked about sex. Eventually, I figured out that they'd had intercourse because they'd conceived my sister and me. But I didn't understand what the act was all about and their silence made it seem secretive and sinful.*
>
> *My attitude toward my own sexuality was also influenced by certain experiences. For instance, sometimes when I was a little girl taking a bath, I put my hands on my private parts. My mom would yell at me, and tell me that was naughty. I didn't understand and made a negative connection.*

I've talked with other women friends about their experiences. A couple of them were sexually abused. They developed a distorted idea of what sex was all about and haven't been able to shake that off. For instance, Darla was raised in the 'make love, not war' era and slept around before she became a Christian. So she brought a lot of guilt into her marriage. Past teaching and experiences often don't make it easy to see sex as good.

1. Think back to see if past teaching or experience has influenced the way you view your sexuality. Then write a paragraph describing what happened and how it has affected you.

2. Read Song of Solomon 2:5-6, 16-17 to see if you find any indication of strain in Beloved's attitude toward intimacy. Which of the following words best describes her? Fearful or eager? Restrained or free? Guilty or innocent?

3. Jacob and Leah's daughter Dinah, whose experience is described in Genesis 34, had a painful sexual experience. What was it?

What happened as a result? How do you think these events might have affected her?

4. What do the following passages suggest that a woman can do to limit the permanent harm from these kinds of experiences in her past?

🐛 Luke 18:1

🐛 Ephesians 4:32

🐛 2 Corinthians 12:9

5. How do you think a woman who was wrongly taught about her sexuality might be helped by reflecting on the Song of Solomon?

If you were wrongly taught or had sexual experiences that are affecting marital intimacy, ask God to enable you to internalize positive truth during this study.

Friday:
I've gone through life hating machines: lawn mowers, sewing machines, electric tools. Cold, hard, unyielding, and superior—they harbor secrets they've dared me to discover. I've wished I could get along without them. One of the problems has been that my experience with machines has not been good. Instructions to "push lever then twist and pull up," I execute. But nothing happens. Or the machine whirs and chugs and sputters and stops.

Then a generous friend gave me a brand-new, state-of-the-art computer. As a writer, I knew that I *had* to make friends with *this* machine. It had the capacity to greatly simplify my life.

But early experiences leered menacingly at me: *others are mechanically minded; you are not.*

Necessity and a desire to work smarter, not harder, drove me to tackle the instruction book—thick as our phone directory. My benefactor friend ran through commands with me.

Now, after months of work and patience with myself, I've changed my mind. Machines are not members of a steel, enemy army out to defeat me. As a matter of fact, the other day I do believe my lawn mower was smiling at me.

1. In this study, we're challenged to align our attitude toward sex with God's attitude. What does the main point of 1 Corinthians 7:2-4 tell you about the rightness of sexual passion between husband and wife? How does that reinforce your attitude?

2. Read aloud Song 1:2 and 6:3a, substituting your mate's name for Lover. Write a description of your feelings as you did it. What further insight does that give?

3. To line up your attitude about human sexuality with the Bible's is a process. "Be changed within by a new way of thinking," Paul writes in Romans 12:2 (*Everyday Bible*). What techniques, used by advertisers to change our minds about products, could we also use to change ourselves toward more biblical sexual values?

4. Ask the Holy Spirit to energize you as you internalize the fact that *sex is good*. Do so by reflecting daily on James 1:17, recognizing that the words refer to sexuality as well as to other gifts. "Every good gift and every perfect present comes from heaven; it comes down from God." Each day repeat this verse prayerfully to yourself, emphasizing an important word or phrase. Tell God your thoughts when you do so.
    "*Every* good gift and every perfect present . . .
    "Every *good* gift and every perfect present . . .
    "Every good *gift* and every perfect present . . ." (TEV)

23

5. As your mind begins to change about the goodness of sex, look for a way to let your husband know. Will it be with words or actions? Keep in mind that whether or not you're having "good sex" now, sex *is* good.

6. Write the second part of the letter to your husband that you began on Friday of Chapter One. You may want to talk about the following subjects:

   ❧ The way in which the main characters of Song of Solomon are taking on life as real people and what that means to you.
   ❧ How the fact that marital sex is good and was created by God has potential to enrich your lives together.
   ❧ Your feelings as you look at yourself naked in the mirror.
   ❧ Record Beloved's love statement in Song 1:2 or 6:3a and paraphrase it as a love statement to your husband.

JUST YOU AND ME: For Husbands and Wives

❧ See who can come up with the most reasons why sex is good. Talk about how this is different from "good sex."

❧ Talk about references to shoddy ways sexuality is represented in what you see or hear. Discuss whether you need to take steps to expose yourselves to less of these influences.

❧ Put a flower on or near your bed to signify the beauty of sexual intimacy. Tell your husband what that flower brings to mind.

❧ From time to time, take the initiative to hold his hand.

❧ Talk over wrong teaching or experiences that may interfere with your physical relationship. Discuss ways that you can help one another. Consider whether you need outside help.

COURTSHIP AND ROMANCE
Song of Solomon 1:1-17

JUST YOU AND GOD

My husband and I met on a blind date. John sang to me that night on a moonlit beach, and I fell in love with him.

John lived in Manhattan, and I lived on the eastern end of Long Island. During our courtship, he'd ride the train to see me, and we'd sit on the porch of the house where I boarded. We'd walk for miles down quiet, small town streets, and go for dinner at the nicest restaurant in town.

On my day off, I'd ride the train to Manhattan. He'd meet me in Grand Central Station and show me the city. He'd buy soft pretzels from a street vendor, or a carnation at a flower stand.

We floated like kites through cool evenings. Reluctantly, we hauled ourselves down. In Little Park next to Little Fountain, sitting close on Our Bench, we measured minutes on the clock, one single watchful eye set in the tower of a tall insurance building. A few more ticks and I would have to return to Grand Central Station and home.

We exchanged letters daily. My heart thumped as I walked into my boarding house after work to see if the mail had come. Whenever a letter arrived, I'd race up the stairs to my room, close the door, and sprawl across the bed to read and reread how much John missed me.

Three months after we met, on my twenty-first birthday, we became engaged. Approximately six months after we met, I moved to Manhattan and we were married.

No need to ride the train to see one another now. No need to write impassioned letters at midnight. No need for John to ply me with dinners and flowers to convince me that we belonged together.

But courtship didn't end with the marriage license. On some paydays, he still brought me a rose. When we could afford it, he took me out for dinner. In the evening, he turned the lights low, tuned in music on the radio, and urged me to sit next to him on the sofa.

I liked being courted and certainly didn't want it to end just because we'd signed a marriage license. As I read the definition of *courtship*, it isn't supposed to cease. Courtship is "the act, process, or period of courting, or wooing."

Notice that the dictionary gives us three ways to define courtship: an act, a process, a period. How do you see courtship? As boxes of candy or bouquets of flowers during dating? Or as a process that's meant to begin on a first date and end when Jesus takes us home?

Monday

"Military tattooing?" I frowned as my husband and I passed the convention center where the words appeared on the marquee. "What's that?" I imagined people lined up at booths waiting to have pictures of eagles or American flags needled into their flesh.

John straightened me out. "It's signals or music played on drums or bugles in the military." Just then we saw a contingent grouped outside, bugles in hand, ready to play.

My misperception would have made a good *Far Side* cartoon. But the way we see a subject is limited by the information and experience we have—whether it's military tattooing or courtship.

Our perception of courtship need not be limited to old, narrow definitions of "the way we've always done it." In the past courtship has been practiced in ways completely unfamiliar to us today.

How, for example, do you suppose Adam courted Eve? The Bible doesn't say. But in author Harold Myra's fictionalized version, *The Choice*, the man scooped up a lovely fish and handed it to her, the couple swam nude and romped together in the water, he took her to a garden he had crafted.

Earlier in our era, couples practiced "bundling," or climbing into bed together completely clothed. This custom probably started because servants had no place of their own to meet. Besides, in cold winters without central heating, the poor had trouble finding warm locations to court. For the sake of propriety, some cultures even used a *bundling board*, a foot high piece of wood placed right down the middle of the bed!

Today we woo by gadget—whispered telephone conversations, a heart-felt fax. Some people even use skywriting and billboards to say "I love you." The point is that what courtship *has been* to us isn't necessarily what it *needs to be* to us now. The only prerequisite is that lovers touch one another in the depth of their souls.

1. Read chapter 1 of Song of Solomon and list ways Lover and Beloved court one another.

2. To whom is Beloved speaking in 1:1-4? How would you describe her tone? What emotions does she reveal?

3. Who has been taking the initiative in your intimate relationship? If a pattern exists, describe briefly what it is and any changes that need to be made. Ask God for insight and direction.

4. What words and phrases make 1:1-4 a romantic speech? How is repetition used for emphasis?

Note: Kisses were a common way of greeting and parting. When done formally, it was much the same way today's Middle Eastern people grasp each other by the shoulders and kiss each cheek. This signified relationship between family and friends. Of course, lovers also practiced more romantic kisses as well.

Wine was an important part of the life of Jews. It was used in worship, as a drink in daily life, and was associated with godly celebration for the Lord's goodness.

The word for "perfume" is literally "incense." Perfume was widely used in Bible times. In a hot climate where one perspired profusely, (and water was scarce) it was especially important and was applied to head and hands as well as the body.

5. Write verses 1:2-3 in your own words. Now rewrite how you might say the same thing to your husband. How would you feel about saying that? Talk over with God anything that comes to mind.

Tuesday
Why do you suppose that women's magazines often feature articles telling how to hide a woman's physical flaws? Probably because so many of us have flaws to hide. It may be that we have almost no bust, an abundance of hips, too high a forehead, or too broad a nose.

As a young adult, I always felt flawed—not because of physical characteristics but because of an overpowering sense of personal inadequacy. So when the wonderful, handsome, talented man who became my husband fell in love with me, I was stunned. Because others had rejected me (and I was afraid John might also), during my early years of marriage, I generally tried to go along with whatever he wanted. I was afraid to express my own ideas and feelings. Not an ideal way to develop an adult relationship.

Articles in women's magazines urge us to camouflage our defects. And that's OK so long as our "defects" are physical and we realize that everyone's body is out-of-kilter. Having a long nose or big ears is part of being human; it doesn't mean we're weird.

But if the reason we feel inferior is because of internal feelings of inadequacy, a cover job just won't do. We'll be so busy concealing that we won't be able to be revealing. And it's out of knowing and being known that intimacy grows.

1. Why, according to Song 1:6, did Beloved feel inferior? What caused her condition? Was there anything she could do about it?

Note: Vineyards were plentiful in the nation of Israel. The cultivation and protection of vines was hard work. During harvest every hand was put to work. But it was also a time of singing and celebration.

2. Consult other translations of Song 1:6b, "my own vineyard I have neglected," and write what this represents. If you were having a neighborly visit with Beloved, what would you say to her on the subject?

3. Lover reassures Beloved of her attractiveness in Song 1:8 and 1:15. What word does he repeat for emphasis? Write complete phrases from these verses that indicate how he sees her.

4. In what ways have you felt inferior during your marriage?

Read Ephesians 1:3-6. Write statements from that text that sum up the way God sees you.

Ask God to align your self-image with the biblical description. Spend time in meditative prayer using phrases from the prayer of Ephesians 1. Ask God to help you see yourself as He sees you.

5. Do you think that your husband feels inadequate in some way? Write down ways you can affirm him.

Wednesday
In order to have satisfying physical intimacy, we must set the mood. Sexy evenings don't just happen. They are orchestrated.

It was easy for Solomon and his bride to set the mood. They had musicians and the finest foods and lavish accouterments available. But unlike Solomon and his bride, you probably don't have a stream of servants running interference for you. There's no one to mop up the spilled milk and clean up after the dog but *you*.

The average woman living in Solomon's day didn't have much help either. In fact, most families lived in one-room houses. In the front section, animals slept at night. At the rear of that room was a raised stone platform — where everyone ate and slept.

Instead of music, the couple was likely to bed down to the sounds of woofing and baaing. Not much chance at 144 Bethany Way to set a romantic mood. At least most of us today have our own bedroom with a door we can *close*, a radio or stereo, a bed instead of a mat on the floor. Think of the possibilities!

1. In chapter 1, Lover and Beloved set the mood for romance by what they said to one another. What endearing term did Solomon use in Song 1:9? According to the context, what was his tone?

   Write several ways to say something similar to your husband.

2. Myrrh, mentioned in Song 1:13, came from the wood of a fruit-bearing tree with white flowers that women wore as a sachet of fragrance around their necks. Henna (verse 14) was a yellow-white blossom. This plant made orange-red dye. Explain why Beloved's statement in these verses is romantic. What similar items common to your life could you use to describe *your* lover?

3. To what prized item does Solomon compare Beloved in Song 1:9? What additional meaning do you draw from the fact that only stallions pulled chariots? (Take into consideration the effect a mare might have had.)

4. Finish the following statement in which you compare your mate to your most prized possession. "Darling, you mean more to me than . . . ." How might such words affect him?

5. Another way that Beloved romanced Lover was by looking her best. According to Song 1:10, what is one way that she did that? Rate on a scale of 1–10 the care you take of your appearance when you're at home. Is your appearance at home likely to contribute or distract from romance? Ask God to help you develop an unselfish attitude about the way you look at home.

Thursday

I was driving with two new acquaintances to a retreat center where I was to speak. The conversation turned toward our marriages. "She kidnapped her husband!" Jill said of our companion, Deserie.

When I gasped, Jill laughed and explained. "She surprised her husband by making reservations for the weekend at a resort, arranging things at home, and packing the car. Then she picked him up at work and whisked him away without telling him where they were going."

I had to wonder about his response.

"After he got over the shock, he was thrilled," Deserie recalled.

Deserie is definitely a major contender for the "Romancer of the Year" award. Many of us, though, couldn't manage such a splash. It's hard enough for us to engineer an evening alone at home and find money in the budget for special food. Big splashes are out of the ordinary. Even my friend Gary, who rented a limo for his beloved and himself and ordered it driven to stores where he bought her expensive gifts, has done so only twice.

Does the fact that we *can't* manage dashing experiences mean we should do nothing to romance our husbands? Of course not. We simply decide what we *can* do. Decorate the bedroom with red hearts and black lace? Urge him to sit next to us at the window and enjoy the full moon? Extend an invitation to take a bubble bath together?

What do you think your husband would enjoy? Given your budget and schedule, what will work for you? Discovering what we can manage and make happen today is what counts.

1. Getting and keeping a husband was vital to women in Solomon's day. Almost no opportunities existed to have careers. How does Abigail's attitude in 1 Samuel 25:39-44 illustrate that?

2. Because some women are more independent and view marriage differently, they may view the idea of creating romance in marriage as an option rather than a necessity. How does your desire for independence affect romance in your own marriage?

2. Which of the following reasons have kept you from been more romantic toward your husband?

   –Not enough money
   –Not enough time and energy
   –Few opportunities
   –Not my job
   –Disinterest on my part
   –Disinterest on his part
   –In a rut
   –Idea is foreign to me
   –I'm angry at him

   Read Proverbs 2:1-6 and pray, as the Holy Spirit leads you, about your response to the list above.

3. Read Genesis 28:1-6 and 29:9-12. In a time of arranged marriages where love came later, what was different about this couple? Describe Jacob's response to Rebekah? Why is this scene romantic?

4. Kisses were used for a variety of purposes in Bible times. Decide the significance of a kiss in the following passages:

   ❦ Song of Solomon 1:2
   ❦ Genesis 29:11-13
   ❦ Exodus 4:27
   ❦ Psalm 85:10
   ❦ Luke 22:47-48
   ❦ 1 Corinthians 16:20

   What kinds of kisses do you give your mate?

5. Kisses don't cost anything, and they don't take much time. How do you think you can better use kisses as a way to create a romantic mood with your mate?

Friday
"I know Ken has something in mind when he suddenly starts paying attention to me and talking sweetly," Joan said. "He doesn't under-

stand why, but instead of turning me on, that turns me off."

Here's how the English dictionary describes what Ken is doing. "Respectful or flattering attention paid to someone in order to get something." That's one definition of *court*. Lobbyists do it in the corridors of Congress; politicians do it on the campaign trail.

We call it "shining on." Carefully staged tête-à-têtes that are out of character yet designed to produce "good sex" tend to make us feel like nonpersons. It's not courting or romancing that's wrong. But effective romantic interludes aren't craftily designed to *create* intimacy. They *grow out of* intimacy that the couple works hard to maintain through communication.

1. Imagine that Beloved is telling a confidante that Lover is not the kind of person who pays attention to her simply to "get something." What do you see in the poem that would make her say that?

2. Song of Solomon 1:16-17 may mean that Solomon built Beloved a private house with prized cedar beams. Or it may mean that she sees the out-of-doors as their bedroom. Which idea does your translations support? Which appeals to you most?

   Note: Cedar was fragrant and one of the finest wood for the purpose of building.

3. Notice that in Song 1:15-17 the man and woman are having a conversation, the man speaking and the woman answering. Why would the kind of dialogue described there enhance intimacy?

4. Wealthy people's beds in Solomon's day were often canopied and luxurious. Without much expense, what is one thing you could do to make the bed where you and your spouse are intimate more romantic?

5. "Be completely humble," Paul wrote to the Ephesians in 4:2. Reflect before God how your practice of humility could bring you and your husband closer. Write your thoughts in the form of a prayer.

6. Write the next section of the letter to your husband. You may want to address the following issues:

- Feelings about taking the initiative in sexual relations
- Kisses you enjoy most
- A desire to know and be known on a deeper level
- Dreams that you have of being alone together

JUST YOU AND ME: For husbands and wives

- Reminisce together about romantic, funny, memorable times in your premarital courtship.

- How satisfied are each of you with the level of intimacy between you? If intimacy is a problem, decide what course of action to take. For example, you could talk with a pastor or qualified Christian counselor; or find a book about intimacy to read together.

- If personal self-consciousness keeps you from enjoying closeness, prayerfully bring up the subject. Help your husband express any self-doubt he may have. Discuss ways you can help one another.

- If you both tend to let your appearance go when you're relaxing together at home, discuss ways you can be comfortable and still appealing.

- Ask what his idea of a romantic evening together would be and tell him yours. With these ideas in mind, plan an evening the two of you can make happen.

WHEN PASSION IS PURE
Song of Solomon 2:1-17

Just You and God

"I know in my head that human sexuality is good because it was created by God. But when I go to bed with my husband and we become passionate, it's a whole other matter."

Jill was expressing the anguish of many Christian women I know. Their whisperings go something like this: "Passion frightens me. I feel as though I'm away from God if my husband and I express our sexuality with abandon. It seems so base and carnal."

"It's not that I don't know that God created sex and it's a gift to us. But how do I convince myself of that when I am the one experiencing the feelings? Sometimes during the month, I have increased desire and I wonder about that too."

"Is the free expression of sexual passion with my husband OK? Is it more than just OK? And if the passion that goes with sex is good, how do I convince myself of that? I'd love to be able to enjoy sex to its fullest, to be all the wife to my husband that I can be."

Monday
"It made me so angry. I wanted to run over and snatch the child away from the woman who had him in the shopping cart. I wanted to ask that mom if she had any idea that she was destroying him." My friend Lana was full of emotional energy. When she began to speak, her words sounded as though they came from the pit of her stomach.

Lana had been shopping in a department store when a woman and a little boy caught her attention. "The woman was shaking him and slapping him and screaming in his face. He just cowered.

"The experience happened days ago, but whenever I think about it, I still get angry and feel badly that I didn't *do* something. But I didn't know what to do."

Lana felt even more passionate about what she'd witnessed than I would. Lana had endured verbal abuse as a child. When she sees another child treated in the same way, her own feelings boil over.

One of my own passions is the suffering of mentally ill people who live on the streets. That's because, for a period of time when I was a child, my own schizophrenic father lived on the Bowery in New York.

When someone makes a remark about "those bums who live under the bridge in our city," my spine stiffens and my stomach churns. My strong feelings motivate me to say, "Wait a minute. Some *bums* aren't just lazy people who won't work. They are mentally ill." My strong feelings don't subside easily, either. Slowly, like a fire ebbing into glowing coals, they are ready to flare when more fuel is added.

1. How does the English dictionary define *passion?*

We know that passion can be good as well as evil. Your strong feelings about social issues, for example, are good. Number the following issues in the order of your concern:

_____ The homeless
_____ abortion
_____ abuse
_____ world hunger
_____ the environment
_____ crime

2. Your capacity to feel passion—including sexual passion—is God-given. Read the second chapter of Song of Solomon and list at least five phrases that, in your opinion, reveal strong sexual desire.

Choose one of these phrases. Use it in a love note to your husband.

3. Read Song of Solomon, chapter 2. In 2:1 Beloved describes herself as a common meadow flower. In verse 2 Lover makes a different comparison. How does it express his strong feelings?

Note: The Rose of Sharon was a wild, bulbous flower. The Lily had a large blossom and was used to symbolize beauty. It was one of the designs used in Solomon's temple for decorative purposes.

List three statements Beloved makes about Lover in verse 3. Paraphrase and summarize what they reveal about her feelings.

4. My own sexual passion makes me feel:

My Feelings	Often	Seldom	Never
Guilty Ashamed Furtive Afraid I'll lose control Delighted Thankful			

5. Recall passionate times you've experienced with your husband. Then write out Genesis 1:31a. Talk over with God your deepest feelings and ask Him to help you see your own sexual passion as good.

Tuesday

Since your bosom is becoming more buxom and your hips more hippy, you decide that you simply must lose weight. For the next few days, you choose carrot sticks instead of chips and apples instead of donuts.

Then you're invited to a buffet restaurant. You pass up the rich dressings and fried chicken. But at the dessert bar you spot strawberry shortcake of magazine-cover quality. It allures you with its gleaming red berries and puff of white cream.

You pause. You debate. You rationalize. You reach out guiltily. Back at the table, you alibi. *I just couldn't resist.*

That moment at the dessert bar, the memory of all the luscious bites you ever had caused you to salivate and reach out. That was *passion.*

Ordinarily, an encounter with strawberry shortcake would have been a delightful memory. But not this time. Instead, your memories reek with guilt.

1. What are your first impressions when you hear the word *lust?* Now look up the word in the dictionary.

   What definitions are positive?

   What definitions are negative?

2. Describe the process in which a desire becomes evil. (See 1 Corinthians 10:6 and James 4:1-3.) Imagine you had to explain this to a friend who is confused. Read James 1:15-16 and outline what you'd say about this passage.

3. Read 2 Samuel 11:2-5 and explain why David's passion was sinful and Lover and Beloved's was not.

4. Read 1 John 1:9. If there have been times when you've deliberately had sex with a man not your husband (whether before or after marriage), what help does this passage offer?

   According to John, what action can you take? If you want God's forgiveness, take that action now.

   What two promises does God make?

Thank God for His work and tell Him why you know you can count on Him to keep His promises. If you've asked His forgiveness for these same sins before, have self-recriminations returned? Talk with God and resolve them.

5. Choose one of the following and jot down ideas for a short story in which the main characters face sexual temptation. Tell why and what they do about it.

   🐛 Jean's husband is short-tempered, and she meets a man who's gentle and a good listener.
   🐛 Katie, whose husband has gained fifty pounds, is partnered at work with a handsome athletic type who likes her.
   🐛 Twila's husband isn't a Christian, so she leans on a man from church for help. She phones him to come over when she needs direction.

Wednesday

Eve was the last woman to go into marriage with complete innocence. That's true not only because she was without original sin on her wedding night, but because she was completely naive. Not once had she seen a photograph of a couple in a suggestive pose. Never had the girls around the well whispered to her about sex.

Ever since, except for maidens who, like Rapunzel, were sequestered, complete naiveté has fallen into obscurity. It couldn't have existed for young girls of Bible times who slept in the same room with Mom and Dad.

Today, if a girl views only one episode of a soap, she's likely to lose her innocence. Society has made it virtually impossible for a woman's view of the passion of intimacy to remain unsullied. Of our era, one Bible commentator says, "Sex began to invade our streets, our homes. . . . It smeared our movie screens and even started to ooze out of our telephones."[1]

So, instead of the purity of passion we began to think of sex as purely passion. Love became lust and desire became degeneracy because our senses were overwhelmed by the serpent's propaganda. We hear that *Man is a higher form of animal and sexuality is an animalistic urge simply to be satisfied.*

But sin isn't all that distorts our vision. The woman inside the wedding gown has had experiences that distort her vision. She may have seen pornographic magazines or films. She may have tried to purge her mind, but the thoughts and feelings won't leave.

Virginal or not, her psyche is probably not as pristine as her wedding gown. Because that's true of most of us, we need to hear and receive the back-to-basic truth that Lover and Beloved model.

1. Beloved describes strong sexual feelings in Song 2:5-6. Here's how *Today's English Version* translates it:

> *Restore my strength with raisins*
> *And refresh me with apples!*
> *I am weak from passion.*
> *His left hand is under my head*
> *and his right hand caresses me.*

What does this quotation suggest about the power of such feelings?

Note: Raisins, made from dried grapes, were formed into cakes and considered a sweet treat. The apple tree probably didn't grow well in Israel, so most scholars believe that the tree here is apricot.

2. If Solomon had viewed sexual passion as sordid, what different tone would you expect to find in this poem?

3. Song 2:7 is the refrain and is repeated in 3:5 and 8:4. Do you agree with the following interpretation? "Beloved reminded all those desiring a relationship like the one she and Solomon enjoyed to wait patiently for God to bring it into their lives."[2] Why or why not? Consult other translations. If you agree, in what way does it indicate that passion is pure?

4. What past experiences caused you to lose your innocence? In what ways do they affect you now?

40

5. God tells how to regain a biblical view of our erotic feelings in Romans 12:2a and Ephesians 4:23. What main idea is common to both passages?

How does it apply to question four? Turn this principle into a prayer and repeat it frequently.

Thursday

Picture it: a sign posted in front of The First Temple of Canaan. ORGY TONIGHT: A *Worship Experience. Be There.*

For the Canaanite neighbors of Israel, such events were as common as Christian potlucks are to us. "At temples scattered throughout their land, Canaanite worshipers actually participated in lewd, immoral acts with 'sacred' prostitutes."³ It was erotic worship designed to persuade Baal to bestow fertility in all its forms.

The Canaanites (and other Mideastern cultures) viewed sex entirely differently from the view that God had revealed in His Laws to His people. In Jehovah's kingdom, intercourse was to be limited to marriage. Further, no Israelite man or woman was to become a temple prostitute (Deuteronomy 23:17).

Human sexuality was not to be used simply to satisfy a physical urge—as though one were shoveling down a burger and fries from a drive-in window. Neither was it to be used to worship the god of fertility.

Sex was to be reserved for the binding of husband and wife. *Inter* means "between or among," and *course* means "movement." So *intercourse* is "movement between two people."⁴ It is God's way for every Adam and Eve to *know* one another—the word that is used in the Bible instead of intercourse. Here's how a pastor friend explained it. "God didn't use the word *know* because He was too shy to use *intercourse,* but because the word *know* denotes the most intimate relationship, connection, and union that there is.

Joe Canaanite and Joe Cool may try to redefine sex according to their lust—to sever passion from its purpose. But they only demean and destroy.

1. How did Shechem sever passion from its purpose in Genesis 34:1-2?

41

If you were Dinah, how do you think you'd feel about the incident and Shechem's feelings in verses 3-4?

2. The Greek word *ginosko*, which means "to know," shows a relationship or connectedness. How is that word translated in Matthew 1:25? (Consult more than one translation.)

Brainstorm as many ways as you can that contrast the Matthew concept with Shechem's view of sexual passion. Ask God to keep helping you see sex as part of *knowing* your husband.

3. In Song 2:8-9, Beloved describes Solomon coming to see her before her wedding. Based on the verbs in this passage, write instructions for an actor playing this scene. Explain how Beloved's description of Solomon would influence the selection of the actor who'd play the role. What attitude does Solomon's actions reveal?

Note: A stag is a mature male deer. A gazelle is a small variety of antelope with lovely, dark eyes. They are fleet-footed; young ones were made pets.

4. What feelings do you have as you read about the walk on which Lover takes Beloved in 2:10-13? What words and phrases create the mood? Write adjectives that describe the experience.

5. On their walk, Solomon and his Beloved have a chance to know one another intellectually, emotionally, and spiritually. What are some ways that you can create more opportunities to do that in your marriage?

Friday
A few dozen Southwestern teenage males made the headlines because they formed a "sex club." Members gained points for every girl with whom they had intercourse. If a guy was intimate with the same girl more than once, it didn't add extra points.

"Do you care about these girls?" a TV interviewer asked.

"Of course," one answered.

Can you imagine a similar interview with Solomon? "Do you love all these women, your Majesty?" We can only speculate his reply.

What do you think? Is it possible to love more than one partner? Is it possible to have sexual intimacy as an expression of love with more than one partner?

It is—if one defines *love* as affection or desire. But that's not how the Bible defines it. In the Old Testament, several Hebrew words are translated "love." Their meaning is defined more precisely by the context. Most of the time, it implies commitment, a willingness to practice fidelity and to weather life together.

That's the relationship out of which coitus is to spring. *My love is so powerful that I want to be with you as long as I live. I want to be legally, morally, and spiritually committed to you alone. Therefore, I give myself to you in this most intimate of ways.*

In God's eyes, sex and marital love are joined at the heart. Passion was designed to express that unity. No way is it merely a casual surge of feeling like the thrill of a carnival ride. Instead, it is an ecstatic celebration.

1. The Greek word *agape* is often used in the New Testament to mean "a deep, self-sacrificial love," and is based on God's own love. First Corinthians 13:4-7 describes fourteen qualities of that love. Which of the qualities mentioned in 1 Corinthians 13 are most evident between Solomon and Beloved?

In what ways does this love reflect marital commitment and fidelity?

2. Read Song 1:15 and 2:14a. Explain why you think a dove is an appropriate symbol for Solomon to use in describing his beloved one.

What features in her does he find endearing? (See Song 2:14b.) Do you think Solomon is being sincere or flattering? Explain your view.

3. What main point is Beloved making in Song 2:16a?

Record the word pictures she uses in Song 2:16b-17 and what they mean. How would you expect a contemporary writer to express these ideas?

4. Read Song 2:15 keeping in mind that foxes destroyed vines by digging at their roots. What foxes might erode Lover and Beloved's commitment?

Which ones recur in your own marriage?

5. Write thoughts you'd include in a letter to your soon-to-be married daughter about sexual passion as an expression of love. Draw from what you've learned in this chapter. Then turn those thoughts into a personal prayer for your own marriage.

6. Write the next section of the letter to your husband. You may want to address some of the following issues:

   ❦ The pleasure of the sexual passion you've experienced together
   ❦ Anything new you've learned from this study about lust
   ❦ Solomon and Beloved as role models in the expression of pure passion
   ❦ The joyous potential of using sexual intimacy to *know* one another in the deepest sense by giving ourselves to one another.

JUST YOU AND ME: For Husbands and Wives

❦ Tell one another one issue about which you have strong feelings. Then discuss how you both feel about expressing the same passion during sex.

❦ Wear something purple and let your mate know that it's the color of passion.

❦ Talk about early experiences that colored the way each of you came to feel about sexual passion.

❦ During sexually intimate times, experiment with new ways of touching, such as stroking and caressing.

❦ Sexual intimacy has been called a sacrament. Discuss what you both think about the idea of praying before or after intercourse.

THE LANGUAGE OF LOVE
Song of Solomon 3:1–5:1

JUST YOU AND GOD

Daddy was Jewish; mama was Christian. Daddy became mentally ill and was institutionalized when I was two years old, making mama a suddenly single parent.

Mama and I lived in a Jewish neighborhood in Brooklyn: Coney Island. There, I observed the Jewish family life I had missed.

Especially, I remember husbands and wives. "My Morris," the lady upstairs would say. "He works nights. So hard he works. So hard to sleep during the day with all the noise."

"My Abie," the lady next door would purr. "See what he bought me? Such a man!"

I heard couples complaining and cajoling, much like Tevye and his wife in *Fiddler on the Roof.* I saw their knowing smiles. Warm touches. Playful smacks on the fanny.

Memories of my Brooklyn days taste as rich as hollandaise. The bits of events form an auditory imprint: the complaining, cajoling, bragging, or mothering—sometimes volatile, always rich and vibrant. These vivid, bold strokes paint an arresting portrait. Gentiles I knew outside this Coney Island enclave paled in comparison.

They may not have spoken perfect English, these Jewish wives of my childhood. But, with their words and gestures, they communicated in a universal language that only now do I understand. It was the language of marital bondedness, of commitment. It was the language of love.

Monday
Time: about 5:30 P.M.
Place: my home.

I'm standing at the counter preparing dinner. Out of the corner of my eye, I can see our dog, Puppy, sitting in the utility room staring intently at the back door. *My master's coming.*

She hears his car pull in the driveway. *Waggle, waggle.* First her tail and then her whole body.

My husband John climbs the back steps. Now Puppy is on her feet, dancing and woofing hello. *I'm so excited, I can't stand it.* John unlocks the back door and opens it.

"Hi Pup. How're you doing?"

She jumps at him and waggles in a circling dance. He stoops and ruffles her fur. She dances beside him into the kitchen.

How it was that she knew when the main event of her day would take place, I cannot say. But because she knew, she was able to experience the pre-pleasure that can be nearly as exciting as the whoopie itself. We call it anticipation.

1. Anticipation over an event often makes us so excited that we dream about it. Imagine you are Beloved telling about your dream in 3:1-4 and write what you'd say.

Note: For protection of inhabitants, a watchman guarded the city gates.

2. Read Song of Solomon, chapter 3. What similar phrases does Beloved use to refer to Solomon in 3:1, 2, 3, and 4? What does the repetition imply?

What other feelings come through in 3:1-4? What do you think they reveal about her inner thoughts?

3. Her mother's house, to which she took Solomon in her dream, was probably the place she felt most safe. What does that and her other action in verse 4 reveal about her?

4. What recurring dreams do you have about your husband? Write about any significance you think these dreams may have, then talk with God about what you see.

5. Describe the anticipation you felt early in your marriage about being with your husband and then the way you feel now.

Reread 3:1-4 to sense Beloved's mood and write about similar feelings you'd like to renew.

Tuesday

Your wedding day. How much can you remember? What you and he wore? What members of the wedding party wore? The music? Words spoken to you during the ceremony?

One thing you probably do recall plainly: the momentousness of the event—because life with the one you loved was about to begin.

If you had lived in Solomon's day, you'd be likely to remember every detail of your wedding because it would be one of the greatest celebrations in your life. Your betrothed, accompanied by friends, would lead a procession to your parents' home and escort you to the place where you and he would live together.

Your wedding would have been as lavish as parents could make it. The bride and groom were king and queen for a day.

Not many weddings though were as grand as Solomon and Beloved's. Imagine the bride who was probably dressed in a finely embroidered white robe, a girdle, jewels braided in her hair, and a garland atop her head. See her carried in the procession on a luxurious litter-bed by her husband-to-be's powerful men.

At most weddings, musicians traveled with the party, creating melody and lyric. At Solomon's wedding, the sound would have echoed across the desert as the group made their festive way to the palace.

At the ceremony (which was civil, not religious), it was traditional for the ancient blessing to be spoken:

Our sister, may you increase
to the thousands upon thousands;
may your offspring possess
the gates of their enemies
　　　　　　　　　　—Genesis 24:60

For at least seven days, guests would feast. While the couple honeymooned, guests had responsibility to examine the wedding night sheets for evidence of the bride's virginity.

Village or palace, weddings in biblical days sent an unmistakable message: celebrate with exuberance; this is one of the most wonderful moments of life!

1. Assume that you've been assigned to write an article for the newspaper describing the royal wedding. Using information in Song 3:6-11, what would you say to emphasize its color and pageantry?

Note: at the front and rear of a wedding party, someone swung a container of incense. Solomon's carriage is described as a "traveling couch" by Joseph C. Dillow. "This traveling couch was a box litter with poles projecting from the front and back and was carried on the shoulders of four to six men. It formed a bed upon which (Beloved) reclined."[1] It was common for the bridegroom to be accompanied by friends, and that is probably the identity of the sixty warriors.

2. Beloved is describing the procession as it approaches. What verbs in verses 7 and 11 reveal her excitement?

What details of the caravan would have impressed this country girl? Why?

3. What key word is repeated in verses 9-10? How does her use of it further reveal her feelings about this wedding?

4. Why would Beloved have felt protected, loved, and cherished? What were your primary feelings on your wedding day?

5 On that day, if you invited God to be part of your union, write about how it was expressed in the ceremony. Talk with Him about ways you've succeeded and ways you haven't. If you were not Christians, write a prayer summing up your desire for God to be part of your marital relationship now.

Wednesday

I grew up never, to my knowledge, hearing the word *penis* or many other correct words for private body parts. They simply weren't mentioned in polite society.

Times changed and, thank God, so did I. These days when a woman comes to me for help with a sexual problem and fumbles for words, I'm the one who fills in the blanks.

Not that I'm a female wonder to make you gasp. It's only that I began to realize a couple of things.

First, I realized that it was not wrong to call a testicle a testicle. The modern trend to use correct sexual language was good.

Second, I realized that I had been operating out of a sense of false modesty and a warped sense of propriety. God *gave* us these body parts and we have rightly affixed to each a particular name. But I had to learn to use that language comfortably.

That took time. At first, when I spoke of a "breast" the word felt like a foreign object in my mouth. But soon I was saying it more confidently and, when it was appropriate, I even talked about *my* breasts.

The task becomes much more sweaty for many of us when we transplant *those words* from a safe, objective environment into an intimate, subjective one. Even in the dark with the man we married years ago, it can be hard to say, "It feels good when you massage my clitoris."

Why is it important to learn to easily use terms like *vulva, ejaculation,* and *orgasm* with our mates? One good reason is that, in doing so, we rescue sexual intimacy from the baseness of "let's get it on" in our relationship and elevate it to the place God means sexual relationships to have.

1. Read Song of Solomon, chapter 4. What words repeated in 4:8-11 suggest that this is the couple's wedding night?

With romantic, even erotic words, Solomon lyricizes the couple's lovemaking. He begins in 4:1 by telling Beloved how beautiful she is. Fill in the following chart of specific compliments that he pays her. Consult other translations. (Note: *Temples* in verse 3 is also translated "cheeks.")[2]

Verse	Body Part	Comparison	His Meaning

Note: Veils that covered hair and face were worn in public by women. Since prostitutes did not wear them because they wanted to entice men, being without a veil was considered improper.

The goats referred to in 4:1 are black with long silky hair that glistens in the twilight sun, according to Joseph C. Dillow.[3]

The red pomegranate with its numerous, edible seeds is a fruit from which spiced wine was made. It was valued and was the pattern for the decoration on the hem of the priest's robe.

The fur of a fawn was soft and enjoyable to the touch.

2. Solomon also writes about sex in Proverbs 5. Scan the chapter to gain the background, then paraphrase the meaning of Proverbs 5:19. What word is used both here and in Song 5:5?

    What does its use in these places imply about our use of explicit terms?

3. What inference to Beloved's breasts does Solomon make in Song 4:6? What do you think is the meaning of this verse?

4. Using 4:1-6 as a pattern, come up with words of lovemaking you could speak to your husband.

5. Write the names of as many male and female sexual body parts as you can think of. Read them aloud. Say them again, personalizing them, as: "*his* penis; *my* breasts." Imagine yourself making love with your husband and using these terms. Ask God to help you outgrow any unhealthy reticence or false modesty you see in yourself.

Thursday

Sensual Christians? To many women, that sounds like another way of saying "carnal Christians. Devoted to the flesh."

But that's not what the dictionary says. Sensual means "of the body and the senses as distinguished from the intellect or the spirit."[4]

The sensory nerves of our physical body are not to be labeled with skull and crossbones. Sensuality is a part of who we are. Sight, touch, smell, taste, and hearing are built-in ways for us humans to experience life. More than that, the senses are ways for husband and wife to experience one another.

To Eastern women, sensuality was *not* anathema. For example, before Esther could go to King Xerxes, she had to complete twelve months of beauty treatments prescribed for his women—six months with oil of myrrh and six with perfumes and cosmetics (Esther 2:12). That guaranteed, to an Eastern king, that she'd be alluring and sensual.

You and I don't have a year to make ourselves sexy. We may not even have twenty minutes. But how about taking two or three minutes before we slip into bed to soften our skin with cream and spray key places with cologne?

1. Read Song 4:8-15 and identify the role the couple's senses play in their lovemaking.

   ❦ With her eyes she has (v. 9) . . .
   ❦ Her scent is (v. 10) . . .
   ❦ Her scent is (v. 11) . . .
   ❦ The taste of her kisses are (v. 11) . . .

   Note: Amana is a mountain peak in the Lebanon range; Hermon is a mountain peak in the north of Palestine.

2. Lebanon may have been Beloved's home (verse 8). What invitation was Lover extending to her? Why is this a romantic passage? How might this verse intensify her feelings toward him?

3. List the visual images Solomon creates in verses 12-15. Reflect on the key words *a garden locked up, a spring enclosed,* and *a sealed fountain.* What factor about Beloved is he describing?

Note: Wealthy people grew lovely gardens that the poor couldn't afford. For one thing, they required water, which was at a premium. Nard was an imported oil from the spikenard plant. Saffron was made from crocus and used as a perfume and flavoring. Calamus was an aromatic grass. Aloe was a fragrance made from the eaglewood tree. Another "aloe" mentioned in the Bible seems to be a product of the lily and was used in embalming (John 19:39).

4. In your opinion, what words and phrases most let Beloved know that she is desirable?

What can you say to your husband during lovemaking to let him know that he is desirable?

5. To better enjoy the senses God has given you during lovemaking, first thank God for each one. Then write a way you'll try using at least one of them.

Friday

John and I culminated our marriage during a weekend honeymoon at the Hotel Robert Treet in Newark, New Jersey. As with every couple, that is the most private of memories.

God's Word expresses that experience best. "They will become one flesh" (Genesis 2:24). The physical joining is symbolic and expressive of our emotional, volitional, and spiritual joining.

Wonder of wonders: God has already prepared the bodies of man and woman to unite physically. He has given us the gift of desire. We want to be close—to touch and caress. We want to have intercourse and experience the God-designed, explosive ecstasy of orgasm.

Here is the meaning of the act of marriage. It is an expression of our joining so passionate that it has come to be called *making love*. It says in a way words never could: "I give myself to you; I am yours. I take you to be my own; you are mine." When man and wife bring that attitude to the marital bed, it gives meaning to the act of marriage.

1. In Song 4:16, Beloved speaks, extending to Lover her invitation to consummate the marriage. What does she call him? What do you think is the significance of these terms?

2. What do you think she meant by the second and third sentences in that verse? Respond with your thoughts on the initiative she took and her passionate desire for sexual union.

3. What point in their sexual union is described by Lover in verse 5:1? How do you know? What three ways does he use to let the reader know that he was completely satisfied?

4. In what ways does the language of Beloved and Lover in verses 4:16 and 5:1 give freedom to sexual expression in marriage?

5. Journal about issues in Chapter 4 that impact you most. Consider the following:

🐞 A need to appreciate my femininity
🐞 To delight in the fact that we can arouse one another
🐞 To see sexual intercourse as giving and union

6. Write the next section of your letter to your mate. You may want to address some of the following issues:

🐞 Memories of your wedding night
🐞 What the Song of Solomon has taught you about using explicit sexual language
🐞 Why you know that Christians are sensual creatures and what that means in your relationship
🐞 Your delight in the way God has designed male and female for one another
🐞 What your husband's lovemaking has meant to you

JUST YOU AND ME: For Husbands and Wives

🐞 Having trouble anticipating being together at the end of the workday? Brainstorm solutions to existing problems.

❦ Make plans to renew your vows (either privately or in a public ceremony) on your next anniversary.

❦ What fictional character do each of you feel like when you get ready to have intercourse? What do you learn from that?

❦ Next time you have sex, give and receive enjoyment by using at least one of your senses in a new way.

❦ Read a book together—written from a Christian perspective—about sexual intimacy. Choose one that includes educational information about male and female sex organs. Use it as a springboard for discussion.

NEW PASSION
FOR OLD MARRIAGES
Song of Solomon 5:2–6:3

JUST YOU AND GOD

My youngest son was the family philosopher. Who could miss the wisdom of one of his favorite sayings?

"Holes in your nose will happen sometimes."

It was his ready answer when life suddenly shifted into reverse gear. Maybe the lawn mower wouldn't work when the grass was ankle deep. Or some dog knocked over the garbage can. It was a kind of code between us that meant *trouble is inevitable.*

When it comes to marriage, trouble *is* inevitable. The author of the traditional marriage vows knew what he was doing when he included the phrase, "for better or *for worse.*"

It happens now, and it happened in Solomon's day.

Imagine that you are a hardworking farmer's wife of that era. Your sister is going to be married and you want a new tunic to wear. Ready-made hasn't been invented yet. It's do-it-yourself-time, from wool to garment.

But before you can dig into your cache of fleece, you simply must mill grain and bake the day's bread. You're almost out of water and that means a trip to the communal well. But no time to stay and talk with the others.

At last you're free to get out the fleece. That's when Yussel comes back from the vineyard and says he needs you to help him pick grapes. Longingly, you finger the wool. You sigh and start off with your husband.

It's too late to start spinning by the time you get home. Maybe tomorrow, you think as you crawl in beside him that night. In your dreams, you are spinning, washing and dying the wool, and weaving it into cloth.

Yussel's crescendo snores interrupt your dream just as you were

57

collecting lice eggs to make scarlet dye. You doze off again, but little Deborah has a nightmare. Then young Samuel has a coughing spell. Yussel, of course, sleeps through it all.

You shake Yussel, calm Deborah, and give Samuel some water. *Will I find time to make my tunic? Or will Yussel and the kids keep me awake half the night and use up what energy I have?*

The wedding will take place in a village three day's journey away. Not so far, except that of course you'll be walking while your husband rides the donkey and you've been feeling poorly lately. If it's that time of the month, you'll be feeling worse.

As a faint patch of dawn shows through your home's single window, you think of your cousin Bilah. *Poor girl. Married to Jake the leathermaker. Because of the dog manure he uses in the tanning process, the smell at their place is so bad that they have to live outside of town. Who can be romantic in a place like that?*

Just then Yussel awakens feeling amorous. Your bones ache and your eyes burn and your head pounds. Bilah will have to wait. You need all the pity you can muster for yourself.

B.C. or A.D.—holes in your nose do happen.

Monday

You stare at the passage about marriage during the Friday morning women's Bible study, but your mind is on the cold memory of last night. Jerry climbed in bed next to you and turned away without so much as a grunt "good night."

You'd hoped this would be the night the two of you could put the stabbing words behind you and renew sexual intimacy. But his heavy breathing told you he was asleep. You lay sobbing silently into the night.

The Bible study leader's admonition of love and kindness and understanding between mates slaps you back to the present. You slam the door on last night and fix a Friday morning smile on your mouth. *No one must know. No one here would understand.*

Unknown to you, a few rows ahead a tidy deacon's wife has slid back to her own remembering place. *Do I have to give in to the kind of sexual practices Jeff wants? They seem so wrong to me. I wish I could talk with someone, but no one here would understand, that's for sure.*

The study is over. The leader chats with women as they leave.

In the empty room, she collects her books, then sits in the front row and stares at the wall and into her own last night.

*Why does Phil choose the middle of the night to grope under the covers?
He knows I have to get up early. How can he be so thoughtless?*

*I feel so guilty teaching a class on biblical marriage when I'm seething
about my own husband's lack of consideration.*

The leader stands quickly. *No use going on about it. Certainly no one
here would understand.*

1. Read Song 5:2-4 and explain Beloved's reluctance to welcome
   Lover into her bedroom. When was it? How do you know that,
   despite her reluctance, she wanted to be with him?

   *Note: The doors of houses were secured from within at night with a
   bar or bolt. The latch-opening was a hole in the door through which
   someone outside could reach and unfasten the bar or bolt unless the
   homeowner had covered it up.*

2. Song 5:2a suggests that Beloved was waiting for Lover. But she
   may have been struggling with resentment over the fact that, as
   king, Solomon often had to be away. List reasons why you've been
   resentful of your mate and decide which are based on legitimate
   reasons and which are not. Pray about what you see and write a
   paragraph of instructions to yourself about actions to take.

3. In 5:2b, Lover spoke as he stood outside Beloved's door with his
   hair wet with the heavy dew of that area. What does the scene
   indicate about the intensity of his feelings? What do you think he
   meant to imply about Beloved by each of the four descriptive
   phrases he used?

4. The couple's sexual relationship was great, but they did fall into potholes. Describe a conversation you imagine they might have about the events in Song 5:1-4.

What kind of conversation would you like to have with your mate about the potholes in your intimacy? Ask God to show you how to have such a talk and write down ideas as they come to you.

5. One of the unspoken struggles many contemporary Christian women have is to know whether or not they should practice oral or anal sex. What if one partner wants it and the other finds it abhorrent? While the Bible doesn't address the issue specifically, what insight do you receive from the following?

Passage	Main Teaching	Insight
Romans 14:7 Romans 14:19 Romans 15:2 Ephesians 5:28		

Based on the above, what are your conclusions?

Tuesday
Today
"Until death do us part"
Sounds like a life sentence.

Too little understanding.
Too little affection.
Too many resentments
Too many disillusionments.
Conflicting emotions
are like odors that do not comingle.
Please,
listen to me carefully
touch me softly
hold me gently.
Conscience elbows:
Your fault.
Apologize. Be alluring.
Sweet. Submissive.
Brain at war with itself.
                                —MD

1. Read Song of Solomon 5:6-8. According to verse 6, how did Beloved feel about her reluctance to let Lover in? What evidence do you have for your conclusions?

2. As was the custom, Solomon had put the fragrance of myrrh on the door handle as a calling card (5:5). How would you feel if he'd done that for you? Why would that have made Beloved feel even worse?

3. It's unlikely that the watchman literally beat Beloved as described in Song 5:7. Compare Song 5:7 with 3:1-3 and give one explanation for the experience.

Her statement about the watchmen may be an analogy in which she's describing her inward state. What do you think that state was?

4. Reread the poem that introduces today's study. When your conscience accuses you because you've been unenthusiastic about sex, what feelings do those accusations generate? Which of the following actions do you take?

   —I analyze my thoughts to see if I'm guilty or not. If I am, I take appropriate action.
   —I keep worrying or get angry or depressed.

   If you need to make changes, what are they?

5. List the verb phrases in Song 5:5-8 that tell what actions Beloved took in order to be reconciled with Lover. What truth from Christ's teachings in Matthew 5:23-24 applies here? Ask God for wisdom to apply it to your own situation.

Wednesday

Christopher and Jonathan (my three-year-old twin grandsons) and their parents left yesterday after a week's visit. Since they live in Illinois and we in Oregon, it's been a year since they were here.

That meant that everything in our house was new again to the twins.

"What's that?" Jonathan asked, pointing to the travel alarm clock on the table.

I explained, demonstrating how it worked.

"Can I touch it?"

We sat down to have lunch. "What's that?" one of them asked, pointing to the cluster of candles in the center of the table.

Mommie explained.

"Where's the fire?" a brother demanded, pointing to the candles and thinking of ones on a birthday cake.

Intimidated by our stereo speakers—apparently because he'd heard loud sounds from some, somewhere, sometime—one of the twins solicited Grandpa's help.

"You touch it."

Grandpa dutifully walked across the room and obliged.

"You hold my hand so I can touch it."

Grandpa and Grandson made the trip across the room, hand in hand.

It was a week full of questions: about ants on a tree, about bees making honey behind glass in a children's museum, about waves on the Pacific Ocean.

The twins weren't so grown up that they thought they should have all the answers.

1. To whom did Beloved go in Song 5:8 for help? For what kind did she ask? Why is it hard to ask for help when you and your mate have a disagreement?

2. Read the following passages and list people to whom we can go when we need help.

Passage	Person	Contemporary Counterpart
Ecclesiastes 4:9-10 Luke 15:20 1 Timothy 5:17 Hebrews 13:17		

Draw a star next to the people with whom you'd feel comfortable talking about a situation that's affecting your sex life.

3. Compare the question Beloved asked in 5:8 with the questions in 5:3 and comment on the differences.

4. Wise friends ask us questions in order to make us think. Why does 5:9 have that affect? Write an imaginary dialogue between you and a friend in which you tell her about a rift between you and your husband. Then form the thought-provoking question she asks

in return based on verse 9. Comment on the imaginary conversation.

5. Do you think that God is willing to give you wisdom in resolving differences that affect your sexual pleasure? Why or why not?

Read Luke 11:9 and Ephesians 6:18a. Notice that these verses speak no restrictions. If that helps you see things differently, write how. Pray about anything in your sex life that is causing problems.

Thursday
Today, I'm on my way home from a weekend as retreat speaker in a lodge at the foot of Mt. St. Helens in Washington State. Because I'd been pressed with work before I came and because my husband wanted me to be as rested as possible, he took me to lunch the day I left home. He rolled up my sleeping bag and bought me a box of granola bars in case I got hungry during the weekend. He assured me that he'd be praying.

I've missed him. Never mind that we've had our sandpaper moments when I rubbed him raw and he did the same to me. When I didn't see how he could say a thing like *that* and he couldn't see how I could possibly say what *I* did. Now I wish we could sit close on the sofa and hold hands.

Lying in my bunk late at night, I recalled other times I've returned home from speaking engagements. The plane taxied into the airport. The seat belt sign went off, and I collected my carry-ons. Stiff-legged, I made my way to the arrival gate.

Always, he was there waiting, looking taller than I remembered. Handsome. Strong, with the smile that still stirred me. Our disagreements were charred cinders to grind underfoot.

He hurried toward me, took my bag with one hand, my arm with the other and kissed me. "Welcome home, Hon."

I responded with my own hug and kiss. "You look great."

As we walked side by side, he told me his surprise. "I fixed chicken for dinner. Your favorite."

What a guy!

1. In answer to her friends' question, Beloved pays Lover ten compliments. Read Song 5:10-16 in several translations, then write the way she might say each one if she were your contemporary.

Note: "Chrysolite was a yellow stone, perhaps the topaz. Marble . . . is extremely hard and capable of a high polish. It is usually white, but is sometimes red or yellow. The Hebrew and Greek words translated as marble means brightness or glistening."[1]

2. Joseph C. Dillow says of Song 5:10-16, "The description that follows has some rather sensuous details that suggest she is reflecting on a previous lovemaking episode with him and pictures him nude in her mind."[2] Do you agree with Dillow's analysis? Why or why not?

3. In which verses in Song 5:10-16 does Solomon use similes — comparisons that include *like* or *as*? In which does he use metaphor — the comparison of one thing to another without *like* or *as?*

Write two compliments about your husband — one a simile and one a metaphor.

4. It's easy to focus on one another's thoughtless times or annoying habits. Reflect on Philippians 4:8 and journal ways your husband demonstrates one or more of these qualities. Look up words in a dictionary if you're not sure of their precise meanings.

5. If a mate's chronic anger controls his behavior, if rifts continually take place, the couple may need advice from a Christian professional counselor. Read 1 Corinthians 12:7-31 and list as many reasons as you can find why it could be God's will for a couple to seek that kind of help.

If you need to take that step, pray for strength and direction. If not, pray that you'll be sensitized to people who do.

Friday
Laura didn't belong anywhere. A bike accident at age 14 left her a paraplegic. Her mother visited her in the hospital and said flatly, "You can't come home." Mom decided that she didn't have time, money, or energy to take care of a handicapped daughter.

For the next three years, Laura was shuffled to seven foster homes, but none allowed her to stay long enough to put down roots. At seventeen, too young to be allowed to live on her own, she found herself sitting in her wheelchair listening to the judge. "I'm going to have to send you to the state mental hospital to live. There's just nowhere else for you to go. It will only be until a foster home opens up."

None did, and she had to stay until she was eighteen, all the while knowing *I don't belong here.*

Laura had accepted Christ as Savior, and He let her know that He loved her. But how could she feel that she belonged to Him when all she had known was rejection?

But as she focused on Scripture, the Holy Spirit began renewing Laura's mind; her sense of aloneness began to fade. She'd tell you now, "I *do* belong. Here, in this apartment. In the lives of friends. But most of all, to Jesus Christ, my Lord."

1. Read Song of Solomon 6:1-3. What statement of belonging did Beloved make in 6:2-3 that she also made in 2:16? What dictionary definition of "belonging" best fits here?

2. Lover had a heavy schedule because he was king. His schedule appeared to interfere with his and Beloved's sex life. Explain the subtle reference Friends make to that in 6:1. How does Beloved's answer in 6:2-3 show that she had adjusted to her position as wife of a king?

3. To belong is a basic human need. Give specific examples of a time when you felt that you didn't belong and a time when you felt that you did. How did you feel each time?

   What phrase is repeated in Genesis 2:24 and Mark 10:7-8 that emphasizes the gift of belonging between husband and wife?

4. When we love someone, we don't want to own them. What kind of love does Ephesians 5:1-2 say we are to have instead?

   List the eight qualities we are to practice in Colossians 3:12-14.

   Choose the three most important in your relationship now, and next to each describe a specific situation in which you can practice it.

5. Of all the virtues mentioned, which seems most important for you to practice now in your marriage? Journal your thoughts to God.

According to Colossians 3:12, we can always be secure that God loves us dearly. How does that knowledge affect your relationship to your mate? Tell God your thoughts.

6. Write the next section of the letter to your mate. You may want to address some of the following issues:

- Wrong ideas you've had about marriage as idyllic
- Tough situations you've made it through.
- The need for Christians to discuss sexual issues more openly
- Good times and not-so-good times to have sex
- Gratitude over the fact that you belong to one another.
- Reflection on the fact that belonging doesn't imply ownership, but allows freedom for personal development.

JUST YOU AND ME: For Husbands and Wives

- Look through ads for lingerie together or go window shopping and ask which he'd like best on you.

- Tell him you'd like his point of view about questionable sex practices. Ask what application he thinks Romans 15:2 has.

- Draw pictures of your most erogenous zones, then exchange and discuss them. Or, with lights out, put each other's hands on those places and demonstrate the most satisfying touches.

- Give yourselves five minutes to make a joint list of reasons why you belong together.

- Review what you wrote on Monday in answer to question 4b and, if God is leading, initiate that conversation.

LOVING FOR LIFE
Song of Solomon 6:4–8:14

JUST YOU AND GOD

Ed and Myrtle must have been married at least fifty years when we knew them. A pioneer family in the Pacific Northwest where we'd come to plant a church, the couple ranched the land they had settled when they were young and strong.

They were still fairly strong, but they were no longer young. Ed continued to tend the cattle and do all the other chores that were a mystery to me. Myrtle kept house. She planted, canned, and froze a mega-garden. Ed hunted. Once, he even shot a bear and gave us some of its meat.

Every morning, their pet mule would come to the back door and bray. Every morning, Myrtle or Ed would gather the leftover flapjacks from breakfast and hand them out the back door to Little Mule. The couple especially enjoyed the amazement of visitors when they witnessed this ritual.

Ed and Myrtle flashed into my mind almost immediately when I sorted through memories for couples whose marriages endured with grace. Clearly, they'd been in for the long haul. The years as settlers surrounded by the Olympic mountains and forest had been sweaty and demanding. Amazingly, though, every blow they endured together seemed to have made both them and their union stronger.

Monday

Doc and the Mrs. are the other couple who came to mind when I rummaged through my past for friends whose marriages could be held up as examples. Doc practiced medicine in a Northwestern city all of his adult life. The doctor's wife suffered cold dinners, canceled plans, and endured middle-of-the night phone calls.

Doc (I never heard anyone call him by his given name) was an oak of a man, and the Mrs. a fragile sapling. When we met them they'd been long retired to house and garden near the shore. They loved Jesus together and knew one another so well that they could finish each other's sentences.

I treasured our visits with Doc and the Mrs. I hid away in my place of shining things the way they praised one another after all the years, the way they smiled softly at one another, and the gracious way they attended to one another. These were like glimpses at gemstones.

Ed and Myrtle, Doc and the Mrs. — two completely different couples, each with their own style. But each had a marriage that had been as carefully tended as Myrtle's garden or Doc's roses. I saw it in their eyes and heard it in their words and came away knowing instinctively that I must tend to my own marriage in order to grow flowers instead of weeds.

1. Read Song 6:4–8:14. Lover romanced Beloved with erotic superlatives even though she had previously rebuffed him. What attitude does he reveal that is also described by Paul in 2 Corinthians 2:5-7?

Note: Tirzah was a beautiful city in the north of Israel.

2. Compare Song 6:4-9 with Solomon's words to Beloved on their wedding night in 4:1-7. List similarities and differences. What conclusions do you draw?

3. Each husband and wife has his or her way of expressing love. Solomon was romantic and verbal. What is your style? Your husband's?

Draw a star next to any of the following areas in which you need to take the initiative to bring freshness to your relationship. Next to them, suggest ways to do so.

❦ Court with little, thoughtful acts.
❦ Express love more verbally.

❦ Plan romantic interludes.

❦ Learn ways to give him sensual pleasure.

4. In your own words, sum up Solomon's statement of love in Song 6:4-9. Why are these words every mate wants to hear? After reflection, write a note to yourself about this.

5. It's easy to take one another for granted and allow communication to deteriorate into disrespect. That chills our sex life. Reflect on Galatians 5:13b and ask the Spirit of God to show you how to apply it to your marriage. Journal what He shows you.

Tuesday

John and I had come to the Pacific shore to celebrate our wedding anniversary. Our apartment on the beach cost more that we were used to spending, but this was a special occasion.

We browsed in little shops, ate at our favorite restaurant, had a between-meal donut at our favorite bakery. Naturally, we walked the beach and sat on a log, talking and sifting sand through our fingers.

Back at the motel, we sat on our private second-floor balcony sipping coffee and watching people below on the beach. As we often did on anniversaries, we reviewed the years, embracing our warmest memories.

After our reverie, we watched vacationers on the beach below. A middle-aged couple searched for treasures, their floppy dog barking and running in circles around them. A younger couple, jeans rolled to the knees, laughed and pushed one another into the surf.

"Look at that girl in the bikini," John directed, and I poked him in the ribs.

"Never mind her. You just pay attention to me—even though I'm past the age of bikinis."

Right below our balcony two men played with two kites—not unusual on that beach with a kite shop nearby. But because of their precise technique, we concluded that they were practicing for a kite flying contest to take place in a few weeks.

They manipulated the strings so that the two kites dipped and soared in duo. The two flashes of color took the wind side by side in perfect harmony, leading and following without falter or flaw—a ballet against sky and sea.

What beautiful rhythm with two gliding as one. How perfect if mates could be just that way through the decades. Always in step. Always in harmony with the other.

I shook my head. We're not soulless, inanimate objects like kites. We're individual human beings with the wills of individuals. To soar in duo we must constantly lay the string back in our Father's hand.

1. Solomon's father, David, says in Psalm 25 that God wants to be our guide. Write the specific phrases from Psalm 25:4-9 that relate to your marriage. Then pray these verses to God.

2. Read Song of Solomon 6:11-13. Although verse 12 is difficult to interpret, it may mean that Beloved is torn between being with Solomon (who was frequently away) and going to her girlhood home. What phrase, repeated in verse 13a by her friends, may indicate that that's the case? If you have other ideas, state what they are.

3. Read Song 7:1-6. Describe the beauty routines Beloved would have continued to practice for Solomon in order to be able to say these words after they'd been married for a long time.

What goals do you need to set for yourself in this area?

Note: The Amplified Version *of 7:2 is helpful: "Your body is like a round goblet, in which no mixed wine is wanting; your abdomen is like a heap of wheat set with lilies."*

The latter may have referred to the color of wheat. The pools of Heshbon were in a city "famous for its fertility and water reservoirs."[1]

The tower of Damascus was for protection of the city and symbolized strength.

4. Verses 7-9 are among the most explicitly sexual in the poem. Paraphrase them and think, before God, about the fact that this kind of erotic language is to be the norm throughout marriage. What does this concept mean to you?

Note: The palm tree is stately and grew as high as one hundred feet, with graceful draping branches. It's dates were a valuable crop.

5. To live in duo, we must let God be our guide, keep ourselves physically attractive and inwardly beautiful as well. Read 1 Peter 3:3-4 and Galatians 5:22-23 and write a word picture of that beauty. Instruct yourself in a spiritual beauty regimen to cultivate these qualities.

Wednesday
Last January, John and I marked forty-five years of marriage. Such an achievement, we agreed emphatically, deserves a really big celebration. A trip *Somewhere Special.*

Months have passed and, for one reason or another, we haven't yet taken that excursion. But we have travel folders and plans. Lord willing, we'll soon step out of *Routine* and head for *Somewhere Special.*

Stepping out of routine has unkinked our relationship more times than I can count. Like every other couple, life has smacked us in the face. There have been illnesses. Unemployment. No money. Disappointment. Disillusionment. Heartache.

Not that a change of geography works miracles. It does, however, allow us to refocus. To shift our fractured gaze from kids and bills and work to you and me and us.

So a couple of times a year, from the time our sons were small, we went away somewhere overnight. In earlier years, I probably spent half the time worrying about the kids, but that still left the other half for *you and me*. And, yes, I'd bring a new nightgown—or the special one I'd saved in the bottom of the dresser drawer.

The main purpose of going to a motel overnight was to shut out the world and be *you and me* again. He'd buy me a bag of cashews and I'd buy him jelly beans. We'd sit and nibble and talk about our yesterdays, our todays, and our tomorrows.

The kids are gone now and our foot-race from their games, to their concerts, to their school open houses has ceased. But still we leave "to do" lists and appointment books behind. We sit and sip and nibble and touch and tell *This is who I am now.*

It's because we are living creatures who are always changing that the necessity to know one another never ends. And *knowing* each other, in every sense of the word, is what marriage is all about.

1. Based on Song 7:11-13, write Beloved's journal entry about the trip she and Lover took together. Include as many details as you can, such as the significance of the season and the purpose of the trip.

Note: The fruit of the mandrake plant was considered to be an aphrodisiac.

2. Now address Beloved in a note giving your feelings about the fact that she initiated sex (v. 12) and made erotic promises (v. 13). Confide to her your thoughts about being that kind of wife as your marriage grows older.

3. Why is the poem's theme in 7:10 especially important when thinking of marriage as a lifetime union? How is it stated differently here from 2:16 and 6:3? What is the significance of the difference?

4. In Solomon's day, public show of affection between members of one's family of origin was considered appropriate—but not between others. In light of this, how would you interpret Song 8:1? Consult other translations. Beloved's reference to family continues in 8:2-3. Write a brief action scene.

5. Reread 7:11–8:3 to stimulate your thinking and jot down ideas for a romantic trip on which you could take your mate. Then list free places you could go for a brief interlude. What would you include to make the trip romantic and satisfying?

Thursday
Lord, past years between my man and me
have been good. Sometimes great.
Terrible too.

It's *terrible* that sticks to my mind like velcro.
When I'm living through a dark day
those memories of *great* are bittersweet
because they were but are not.

Have I expected my marriage to be like a romance novel?
My mate to be all the things my dad and other men
never were?
Have I expected him to handle my ego as though it were a wounded kitten,
soothingly crooning "Poor baby," and "Of course I understand"
infuse me with romantic realism.

I want to accept and be accepted as we are now.
Live life together as it is now.
Sense who You want me to be now.
Please God, I don't just want to be *in* love.
I want to *be* love
to the man who lies beside me.

Let us be only this: two imperfect peas
snuggled in the same pod.

                    —MD

1. If Beloved were writing her testimony, what three problems would she say their marriage had overcome? (See Song 1:5-6; 2:15; 5:2-7.)

   Why did the word *desert* or *wilderness* (Song 8:5a) symbolize trials to the Israelites? What phrase in verse 5a denotes the couples' closeness now?

2. If Beloved's request in Song 8:6a were portrayed in an artist's painting, what do you think it would look like? Write your title for such a painting from the key thought in 1 Corinthians 7:3-5.

   Note: A seal was used to authenticate the signature on a paper as being genuine. It also declared that the item belonged to the person whose seal it was.

3. One of the most powerful statements about love is made in Song 8:6b-7, where Solomon sums up the poem's main message. What do you think that message is? (Note that *jealousy* [6b] can be translated "ardor.")

If you were going to use colors to illustrate this verse, what would you choose? If you were going to set it to music, what melody would you select?

4. Since the feeling of romantic love comes and goes, Beloved must be describing something deeper. Make notes about that love from the following passages and then write a strong statement to guide you in the years ahead.

❦ Psalm 89:1-2

❦ John 10:17

❦ John 15:13

❦ Romans 8:39

❦ Ephesians 5:33

5. As you studied Solomon's poem, what main truth has the Holy Spirit been repeatedly bringing to mind? Review passages through which He's spoken most plainly and write a one-sentence prayer based on what He's shown you. Repeat it frequently as your heart's desire.

Friday
This love poem isn't all Solomon wrote. Scholars have traditionally ascribed to him the authorship of Ecclesiastes as well.

One of the words he repeats in that book most frequently—over twenty-five times, as a matter of fact—is *meaningless*.

> "Meaningless! Meaningless!"
>   *says the Teacher.*
> "Utterly meaningless!
> "Everything is meaningless."
>   —*Ecclesiastes 1:2*

Imagine being married to a man who becomes this disillusioned! You've watched him exercise unparalleled wisdom and super intellect; seen him build coffers of wealth and perform noteworthy feats. But now he's become convinced that none of this has significance. Imagine watching helplessly as he sits depressed, staring at nothing. Imagine caressing him seductively only to receive a wan smile in return.

But you love him, so you wait. Then one day you notice a subtle change. He begins to write what he sees as the wisest of all statements:

> *Remember your Creator*
>   *in the days of your youth . . .*
> *Remember Him—before the silver cord is severed . . .*
> *Fear God and keep His commandments,*
>   *for this is the whole duty of man."*
>   —*Ecclesiastes 12:1, 6, 13*

You smile thankfully to Jehovah. You have your husband back. He's not the man he was. And for that you are grateful as well.

1. So that you can be strong when your marriage is tested, glean principles from Philippians 4:8-13 and write in your own words three guidelines to follow.

2. Draw a circle below. In it, jot words mentioned in Philippians 2:1-3 that create a loving environment in marriage.

Read Philippians 2:4. To which of your mate's interests do you need to be more attentive?

3. In a final scene of this poem, Solomon flashes back to Beloved's girlhood (Song 8:8-9). Her brothers speak. What is their overriding concern? What alternatives do they discuss? Keep the *Amplified* translation of 8:9 in mind. "If she is a wall [discreet and womanly], we will build upon her a turret [a dowry] of silver; but if she is a door [bold and flirtatious], we will enclose her with boards of cedar."

4. What were Beloved's thoughts on the subject? (v. 10) Apparently the vineyard in which she worked as a girl was leased from Solomon by her family, and farmers agreed to certain production quotas (vv. 11-12). What comparison does she make between her marriage and the vineyard?

5. In the couples' final dialogue, how do you know that they were still passionate toward one another? Keep in mind his request (v. 13) and her response (v. 14). What words seem especially significant and why?

How might the instructions in Ephesians 6:10-13 apply to your marriage? Think of particular situations that occur repeatedly and specific actions you can take according to this passage.

6. Write the next section of the letter that you have been creating for your husband. You may want to address some of the following issues:

❦ Reflect on your desire to be role models to younger married couples and what that means to you.

❦ After quoting a heated sexual passage from the Song, tell how it relates to your marriage now.

❦ Write about the love life with your husband that you'd like to have five years from now.

❦ Put down reasons why you appreciate his personality characteristics that are different from your own.

❦ Write about realistic expectations for your marriage.

JUST YOU AND ME: For Husbands and Wives

1. Talk about couples you know whose marriages have endured successfully. What do you learn from the way they relate to one another?

2. Talk about the differences in your personalities and why you appreciate them.

3. Tell your ideas for a romantic trip for the two of you and ask for his suggestions. Set aside time to go.

4. Read Song 8:7 together and discuss the many *waters* and the *rivers* you've survived. Then read 8:7a to one another inserting the personal pronoun "my."

5. Turn off the phone, turn on some music, and cuddle.

THE SONG AS ALLEGORY
Overview: Part 3

JUST YOU AND GOD

On the third finger of my right hand I wear a garnet ring in an old, gold setting. To a stranger it's a pretty and perhaps quaint piece of jewelry. To me, it has a second meaning, because it was a gift from John on our wedding anniversary a few years ago. So it's a symbol of his loving faithfulness throughout the many years of our married life.

When I look at it, I remember the wonder on John's face when he held a son for the first time, his attentiveness whenever I've been ill, the notes he's written to me over the years.

Like my ring, the words of the Song of Solomon—precious and sparkling with love between a man and woman—can symbolize something deeper: the love between Christ and ourselves.

In this chapter we focus on the Song as allegory, with Solomon as a picture of Jesus Christ and Beloved as a picture of ourselves. At first, the explicit sexual language may seem a barrier. To get over that hurdle, we need only remember that the Bible itself gives us permission to compare the love between a husband and wife to the love between Christ and His church.

Passages we'll explore in this chapter will substantiate that. "The spiritual union was *the original fact in the mind of God* of which marriage is the transcript [or copy]."[1] Before launching into the study ahead, review the themes expressed in Song of Solomon:

🌒 Marital eroticism by which a flesh and blood husband and wife express their love in a personal and physical fashion is not tawdry. It is pure.

🌒 Marital eroticism was given us by God, and like all His gifts is good.

🌒 Marital eroticism is an expression of passion for one another and is used in Scripture to illustrate union.

Look behind the erotic language to the love itself. After all, the wonder of love is the underlying theme of the book. Just as marital love binds a couple together, so the love between God and ourselves is the spiritual bond that unites us. The reason we can love at all is because the God who is love created us in His image.

Solomon's poem "gives us language with which to express the love between Christ and ourselves. . . . Love to Christ is the strongest, as it is the purest, of human passions, and therefore needs the strongest language to express it."[2]

Monday

My favorite stories growing up were fairy tales. The thick, hardcover book at my bedside about Snow White and Rose Red, Rapunzel, and those other gossamer girls was one of my early treasures.

Perhaps because I was a child of the depression and welfare, the stories I most often rolled around in my mind were stories about a poor but beautiful heroine. In each tale she faced terrible and seemingly insurmountable obstacles put on her by a powerful enemy. But she was rescued by an even more powerful, absolutely handsome and pure prince.

As I grew, I ached for that to happen. I wanted desperately to be chosen by someone who'd make the girls with whom I'd gone to school take back every nasty word they'd ever said about me.

Women like me who've felt like the most common of commoners hope and pray for a man who will, by the sheer force of his dazzle, say to the world, *She's with me,* so that the world steps back and shows respect.

We imagine those others whispering to one another, "What does he see in her?" We don't care, though, because at least now they're taking a second look at us and searching for what they didn't see before—things that would make a guy like that fall in love with us.

1. In what way does Beloved's position in life as stated in Song 1:6 compare to a Cinderella-type fairy-tale heroine?

2. Reread Beloved's lavish description of her groom in Song 5:10-16. Using the passages below, decide how her words also picture Christ and write a similar description of Him.

Lover	Jesus	Your Description of Jesus
Song 5:11 Song 5:14-15 Song 5:16	Revelation 1:14 Colossians 1:16 John 1:14	

3. What phrases in Song 1:1-4 and 2:3-6 express the prospective bride's strong desire for Solomon?

   Describe your own strong desires for intimacy with Christ. Exactly how do you want your relationship to deepen? Be specific.

4. Read 2 Corinthians 11:2 and explain what *virgin* means in this context. (See Romans 6:17-18 and 1 John 2:15-17 for ideas.)

5. Journal memories of ways in which you made yourself ready to be your husband's bride. What are some specific ways you can prepare yourself to be joined forever with Christ? Journal your response to Him.

Tuesday

As a wedding photographer, it's my son Mark's job to provide filmed memories of the event. With the assistance of his wife Deby, he does a fine job capturing moments and moods so that the bride and groom can recapture years later exactly how they felt.

The brides look the way brides are supposed to look. The grooms? Sometimes a little stunned, but mostly, they appear dashing and unmistakably in love.

If Mark had been hired as photographer at the following weddings, what do you suppose the bridegroom's photographs would look like?

- *Adam, the innocent bridegroom.* He'd never heard of marriage. Until very recently, he'd never even heard of a woman.
- *Jacob, the disappointed bridegroom.* There he was, ready to marry to Rachel, who "was lovely in form, and beautiful" (Genesis 29:17, 18). Through the deception of his father-in-law, Jacob found himself married instead to Leah, her older sister. To tell the real story, in his album there should be photographs of his face when he made the staggering discovery the morning after his wedding night.
- *Solomon, the romantic bridegroom:* poet and nature lover, connoisseur of the finer things of life, monied and titled.
- *Finally, there's the most important bridegroom of all: Jesus Christ.* What kinds of photographs would you expect to find of Him?

1. Choose five words from Solomon's poem that you think best sum up the qualities of Solomon as bridegroom.

Describe the similar relationship you see between yourself and Jesus Christ. Now write five words that tell how that makes you feel.

2. What word pictures do each of the following give of Jesus Christ?

Matthew 12:6

Matthew 13:54

Mark 1:27

Next to each, write something about Solomon that it reminds you of.

3. Solomon's marriage to Beloved reminds us that believers will be eternally united with the Son of God in a spiritual wedding. Look at Isaiah 54:5, Hosea 2:19, Revelation 19:7 and 21:1-4. Write text for a newspaper announcement describing our marriage to Christ.

4. In Solomon's Song, he lyricizes his adoration of Lover and hers of him. Choose a section that most moves you and write it out.

List hymns and choruses that express the same sentiment about the Lord.

5. What is one way our Divine Bridegroom is different from Solomon? (See 2 Corinthians 5:21.)

According to Isaiah 53:5, what has Christ done so that He could become our bridegroom and we His bride? What wedding present would you like to give Him in gratitude? Write your thoughts to Him.

Wednesday
It's testimony time in church and a woman you've never met stands. "I'm learning to know Jesus more intimately than ever." You nod approval. But she goes on. "Jesus has become my lover."

How do those words sound to your ear? Lovely as a field of wildflowers rippling softly in the wind? Or as shocking as a photo of a nude in the church bulletin?

Should a woman see Him as her *Lover?* Webster's basic, one-size-fits-all definition of lover is "a person who loves." He goes on to specify
  a. a sweetheart
  b. a couple in love with each other
  c. a man who has a sexual relationship with a woman without being married to her; paramour
  d. a person who greatly enjoys some (specified) thing."³

Our struggle with the term *lover* stems from the fact that we have been conditioned by society to define the word as "a man who has a sexual relationship with a woman without being married to her." Therefore, we are likely to slam the door on other ideas.

Take a second look. What if you set aside your presuppositions and allow the word *lover* to return to it's origin: "A person who loves." Is it fair to define Jesus and ourselves as "a couple in love with each other?" So what do you think? Is Jesus your Lover?

1. Plainly, Solomon loved his bride and said so in a variety of ways. Review the following passages from the Song and then explain how Christ similarly expresses His love.

Solomon	Jesus
Song 1:9-11 Solomon speaks endearingly.	Matthew 11:28-30
Song 2:14 He desires intimacy.	Matthew 23:37
Song 6:9 He sees Beloved as perfect.	1 John 3:1

2. Besides speaking his love in words, what actions did Solomon take to show his love?

Song 1:11

Song 1:17

Song 5:5

What actions did Jesus take?

John 1:14

Hebrews 4:14-16

Hebrews 12:24a

3. Although we know that God loves the *world*, poor self-worth can keep us from believing that God loves *us*. Read Ephesians 1:3-14 inserting personal pronouns. Then, based on that passage, list at least five reasons why you know that God loves you.

Tell God that you want to wholeheartedly believe in His love and ask Him to work them into your belief system.

4. Solomon certainly wasn't the perfect lover, but Jesus Christ is. Journal about aspects of Christ's love in the following passages: (John 14:23, Galatians 2:20, and 1 John 4:8).

5. "Jesus Lover of my soul, let me to Thy bosom fly,"[4] we sing. In what practical ways can you fly to Jesus' bosom? Do so now.

Thursday
Marriage is not *me* but *us*.
Not *mine* but *ours*.
Our clothes side by side in the closet;
our shoes side by side under the bed.
Our toothbrushes and cologne in the bathroom.
Our plans for the weekend
and this year's vacation
and the kids' college fund
and our retirement.

In the evening we kick back and snuggle on the sofa and say,
"This is living."
We sigh and close our eyes to tomorrow's demands.
Behind our closed eyelids we think
that we're experiencing the best life can afford.
Together
at the end of the day
close
to the one we love.
                    —MD

1. You are developing an ad campaign for the Song of Songs and have come up with these statements:

    ❧ *The couple eloquently sings to one another, "You are my life."*
    ❧ *Their hearts whisper "I am only alive when I am with you."*

    What passages from the Song of Solomon would you use to prove that these are part of the book's message?

2. Suppose you are writing copy for a billboard letting people know that Christ will give us a quality of life that we can't obtain anywhere else. Study Luke 6:48, John 10:10, and Romans 14:17. Then write ideas you'd like to communicate on that billboard.

3. In what way did Solomon give Beloved a life she'd never known?

   Jesus Christ gives us a life we can't obtain anywhere else. He offers us _____ (1 John 5:11), which He defines as _____ (John 17:3). It becomes ours when we _____ (John 1:12-13). It's a _____ (Romans 6:23), and means that we enter into a relationship with God as His _____ (John 1:12).

4. According to John 17:3, why is it correct to say that eternal life begins the moment we become Christians?

   If you were going to celebrate all the gifts you have now as a result of having eternal life, what all would you cheer about? Do so by writing an exuberant prayer of praise.

5. Pretend that you've been asked to give a testimony on the subject, "Christ is my life." Think about it along these lines:

   🍃 He's given me a new perspective.
   🍃 He's given me hope.
   🍃 Because of Christ, I have enthusiasm for life.

   What will you say?

Friday
The man I married has been
an actor
a pollster
an auditor
a minister
a filmmaker
a forensic photographer
But he has never been a king.
One day, though, I am going to marry a King,
And so will he.
—MD

1. Look up passages in the Song where Lover is referred to as king and find one fact in each about his royalty (1:4, 12; 3:9, 11; 7:5).

    How would you feel if you were Beloved and married to so powerful a king?

2. Solomon typifies Christ our King. Read about the Son of God's power and majesty in Isaiah 9:7, Colossians 1:15-17, Revelation 11:15, and Revelation 17:14 and write key words and phrases that describe His kingship.

    In what ways is He superior to Solomon? How does the fact that the Lover of your soul is King make you feel?

3. A king rules over a geographical kingdom. Solomon's kingdom was Israel. Where does Luke 17:21 say the location of Christ's

kingdom is? Make a checklist for kingdom members from the following passages and prayerfully apply it to yourself.

Matthew 5:44-45

Matthew 6:28-34

Matthew 22:37-40

1 Corinthians 6:19

1 John 5:21

4. In the first column, list the phrases that describe the coming of Solomon the King. In the second, list phrases that describe the coming and future reign of Christ the King.

Solomon the King	Christ the King
Who or what accompanies him, Song 3:7	1 Thessalonians 4:16
Way he arrives, Song 3:9-10	Revelation 1:7
Sign of his royalty, Song 3:11	Revelation 14:14

Write your response to the truths that most impresses you.

5. In Song 1:4, what was Beloved's attitude toward the coming of the king? Why are you excited about Christ's return? If you are reluctant, decide why and journal about it.

Memorize Jesus' words in Revelation 22:20a.
"Yes, I am coming soon."

Ask God to develop in you the excitement and enthusiasm over that promise that Beloved had so that you can pray from your heart, "Amen. Come, Lord Jesus" (Revelation 22:20b).

6. Write the last section of the letter you have been composing to your husband. You may want to address some of the following issues:

🐦 Some concepts you've learned about Song as allegory.
🐦 Express desires you have for intimacy with God. Invite your spouse to tell you his.
🐦 Discuss the fact that you'll both become the bride of Christ.
🐦 Reflect on the fact that Christ wants to give you both a quality of life that you can't find anywhere else. Write about ways that idea specifically applies in your relationship.

Reread your letter and make any changes necessary. Prayerfully choose a time to give it to him and to talk together about it.

JUST YOU AND ME: For Husbands and Wives

🐦 Take turns reading the Song of Songs to one another, pausing over passages that provide language you want to use to express the way you feel about Christ. Pray together using that language.

🐦 Recall ways you and your husband acted toward one another when you first fell in love. Then talk about how you felt and behaved when you first came to know Christ personally. What would you like to recapture?

🐦 Each of you answer the question, "If you were king of the world, what are the first five things you'd do?" Are these things Christ will do when He comes? Why isn't He doing them now?

🐦 Do something you both enjoy, and talk about why life is so much richer because you know Christ.

🐦 Shop together for a picture, motto, or decorative item to be a silent reminder that Christ, your King, is coming soon.

Group Guide 1

JUST YOU AND YOU
Overview: Part 1

SING A SONG OF SOLOMON

OBJECTIVE

To see the Song of Solomon as a biblical celebration of marital intimacy

LEADER PREPARATION

1. Read the Song of Solomon in one sitting. Think about why this book is sometimes described as a celebration of marital intimacy.
2. Complete a personal study of *Sing a Song of Solomon*, chapter one.
3. Select a favorite romantic fairy tale or story and decide why you like it.

GROUP TIME

1. What is one of your favorite romantic fairy tales or stories? Explain why you like it.
2. Originally, a "romance" was a piece of literature written in one of the languages derived from Latin. Later it came to mean fiction that included excitement, love, and adventure. What words and phrases throughout this book make it an exciting adventure of love?
3. What value do you think modern men and women might find in this biblical song?
4. Even though the Song of Solomon is a poem, it also contains characters and a loose plot. Give thumbnail sketches of each of the three characters in the Song. (See 1 Kings 4:29-34; 1 Kings 10:23-29; 1 Kings 11:1-6; Song of Solomon 1:1-8; 15, and 5:1b)
5. What visual images most impress you?

6. Do you agree or disagree with early Jews who said this book should not be read by those under thirty? Explain your position.
7. What is one thing you'd like to accomplish during the study of Solomon's song?
8. Look at Genesis 2:25 and Hebrews 13:4 and tell how you think God would define sex. How does it differ from common attitudes in contemporary society?
9. Solomon and his Beloved had flaws, like all humans. But this love poem doesn't dwell on the flaws. Take a moment to think of the good qualities in your own husband. Tell your group three of these characteristics that you appreciate.
10. Read your version of the Valentine message on page 13 that Beloved might write to Lover.
11. Begin a list of "What Every Woman Ought to Know about Marital Intimacy" to be given them on their wedding day. What entries would you include from today's lesson?
12. Offer brief prayers of thanks for your husband. Ask God's blessing on him.

JUST YOU AND YOU

Overview: Part 2

CELEBRATE MARITAL INTIMACY

OBJECTIVE

To see the importance of wooing one another throughout marriage

LEADER PREPARATION

1. Complete personal study of *Celebrate Marital Intimacy*, chapter two.
2. Decide what you think are the most romantic statements in Solomon's poem.
3. Think of a memorable time in your courtship that you are willing to talk about.
4. Imagine ways that busy women of modest means can set a romantic mood.

GROUP TIME

1. What was one of the most memorable moments in your premarital courtship? Why do you feel that way about it?
2. Especially memorable in Beloved and Lover's courtship is the way they talked with one another. Scan Song of Solomon. What statements seem most romantic?
3. A theme of Song of Solomon is: sex is good. What do you think *good* means in this context?
4. Read aloud Genesis 3:1-7. Some people assume that sex and sin are always connected. What evidence do you find in this Genesis passage that the original sin was not sex?
   What impact does Genesis 1:31 have on the subject of sex and sin?

5. In Song 1:2-4, Beloved speaks boldly of her desire. How does her expressiveness compare to the "traditional" role of Christian women?

6. As you reflect on your own marriage, are you able to verbalize your desires to your husband as freely as Beloved did to Solomon? Would this kind of boldness enhance or hinder the emotional intimacy of your relationship? Explain.

7. In your reading of the Solomon text, what indication did you find that Beloved felt inferior? Why? When and why have you had similar feelings?

8. In spite of Beloved's feelings toward herself, how do we know that she was attractive?

9. Go around your circle and have each person admit one characteristic about herself that she knows is attractive. Then go around your circle again and tell one attractive quality about the person on your left. Which trip around your circle was easiest? Why?

10. Why is it important to feel attractive in order to initiate courtship and romance? What are some ways women can make themselves feel that way? What role can 1 Peter 3:4-5 play in your beauty regime?

11. What is significant to you about the fact that Beloved talks about kisses at the outset of Solomon's poem? What are some reasons a kiss between lovers sometimes deteriorates to a peck?

12. If you lived in a one-room home in Bible times, what are some ways you could still act romantically toward your husband?

13. If you were planning a romantic TV series based on the Song of Solomon, what would you include? How do you think TV and film romances influence our own romances?

14. What are some ways that even the most busy woman on a tight budget can court her husband and set a romantic mood. (Be as creative as possible.) Write down one idea and set a goal to try it.

15. What important points about romance would you include in an article titled, "What Every Woman Ought to Know about Marital Intimacy"?

16. Pray together for help in setting priorities, in dealing honestly with things that are keeping you from being a more romantic wife. Ask God to help you create romantic moments that will reflect growing warmth between you and your husband.

Group Guide 3

JUST YOU AND YOU

COURTSHIP AND ROMANCE

OBJECTIVE

To help women see the importance of courtship and romance and actively participate in the process

LEADER PREPARATION

1. Complete *Courtship and Romance*, chapter three.
2. Think of a fictional couple's romance that influenced your expectations and a fictional couple who is a good role model.
3. Be ready to talk about a time when you felt unattractive during marriage so that you can lead others to talk about similar feelings.

GROUP TIME

1. What do you think most determines the way today's women look at the subject of courtship?
2. In view of your study of Song of Solomon so far, do you think that Beloved and Lover see courtship as an act, a process, or a period of wooing? What attitudes of Beloved's toward courtship would you like to adopt?
3. Read aloud Song 1:1-11. Read the paraphrase of Song 1:2-3 that you wrote on page 27. What key thoughts from these passages would you like to communicate to your husband?
4. What couple (real or fictional) have you found to be a good role model?
5. When have you felt unattractive in your marriage? What brought on those feelings?
6. Divide into pairs. Take turns reading Ephesians 1:3-6 to one

97

another as a personal message from God. Then pray together thanking Him for valuing you.

7. Read your version of the statement, "Darling, you mean more to me than. . . ." (Wednesday, question 4, page 30) When might be some opportune times to say that to your husband?

8. Read aloud Song 1:12-14. Imagine you were being interviewed for an article titled, "Twenty-five Inexpensive Ways to Romance Your Mate." Brainstorm with others in your group to come up with as many ways as you can. Include some suggestions for a romantic getaway.

9. Read Song 1:15-16 by having volunteers read the verses responsively in more than one translation. Here Beloved and Lover are having one of their many romantic conversations, but today many couples lack the ability to create intimate communication. What ingredients makes verbal communication intimate? Make a list together to help you remember.

10. What do you think a woman should do if she makes their bed more romantic with satin sheets and soft romantic colors, but her husband doesn't seem to notice or respond?

11. In your continuing article for the about-to-be-married, "What Every Woman Ought to Know about Marital Intimacy," what facts would you stress about courtship and romance?

12. Share one need on this subject and pray for one another.

JUST YOU AND YOU

WHEN PASSION IS PURE

OBJECTIVE

To encourage women to see their own sexual passion a good gift from the hand of God.

LEADER PREPARATION

1. Complete *When Passion Is Pure,* chapter four.
2. List passages from the biblical text in which Solomon uses one of the five senses to create a feeling of sensuality.
3. Come up with ideas for a banner of love Solomon might have designed that also represents the love between you and your husband.
4. Decide what melody best expresses for you the intensity of erotic passion.

GROUP TIME

1. How do you define desire? Lust? Passion?
2. What do you think determines whether these experiences are good or evil?
3. Read aloud Song of Solomon 2:1-17. Study more carefully verses 5-6, 8, and 14-15. Who is speaking in each and what strong feelings does that person reveal?
4. What leads you to believe that the couples' passion for one another was good and not evil?
5. Scan Song chapter two again. In what ways does the poet use the five senses to create a feeling of sensuality?
6. A banner declared the King's royalty. (2:4b) What kind of ban-

ner do you imagine Solomon might have designed to declare his love for Beloved?

7. If it were the tradition to fly a flag to signify a couple's love today, what would you want yours to look like and say?

8. What opportunity does the couple take in 2:8-13 to get to know one another?

9. What opportunities have helped you to know your own husband better?

10. What melody expresses, for you, the intensity of erotic passion? Why?

11. Read Song 2:15. What "little foxes" are most likely to interfere with a couple's free expression during intimacy.

12. Read to each other the letters to your daughter (Friday, question 5, page 45). What points did you stress? Which of these points would you add to your ongoing article, "What Every Woman Ought to Know about Marital Intimacy."

13. How would you describe the way you deal with your own sexual passion? Do you see it as a gift from God? As an expression of your love and commitment? Explain.

14. Spend a few moments in silent prayer about all that you have discussed today, particularly as it relates to your own marriage. Then end your time together with sentence prayers.

JUST YOU AND YOU

THE LANGUAGE OF LOVE

OBJECTIVE
To help women gain freedom to express feelings of erotic love to their husbands

LEADER PREPARATION
1. Complete *The Language of Love*, chapter five.
2. Choose three volunteers to act out the drama in Song of Solomon 3:1-5 and arrange time for them to rehearse during question 1.
3. Think of what your portrait of Song 3:6-11 might look like.
4. Think of an analogy that you could use to express something that you appreciate in your husband.

GROUP TIME
1. Tell about one funny or poignant event on your wedding day.
2. Act out the drama described in Song 3:1-5. What information in the text shows that Beloved was excitedly anticipating her marriage to Lover.
3. What situations can keep a wife from looking forward to seeing her husband at the end of the day? How have you learned to overcome some of these obstacles?
4. Read responsively alternate verses of Song 3:6-11. If you were painting a portrait of this scene, what would you include?
5. How do you feel about the possibility of a thanksgiving prayer before or after intercourse?
6. Read aloud Song of Solomon 4. What body parts did Solomon compliment in this chapter? Why do you think Solomon used

objects like shorn sheep, pomegranates, a tower of David, and fawns as comparisons?

7. Name one physical quality about your husband that you could compliment. What analogy would you use?

8. Did the family where you grew up use correct sexual terms? How have those past experiences helped or hindered you?

9. In what ways do slang and obscene language interfere with the ability to use biologically correct terms?

10. Look again at Song 4:10-15. What references to the physical senses do you find here?

11. Why is it liberating to know that the Song of Solomon encourages the use of our senses in lovemaking?

12. Construct a combined list of body parts from your individual work on Wednesday's question 5 (page 52). Read your combined list aloud in unison.

13. Do you think that the church should encourage the use of specific sexual terms? How and why? (Or why not?)

14. In your continued article titled, "What Every Woman Needs to Know about Marital Intimacy," what points about speaking the language of love would you want to include as a help for the woman who is about to be married?

15. Pray together for God's help as you communicate the language of love in your own marriages.

JUST YOU AND YOU

NEW PASSION FOR OLD MARRIAGES

OBJECTIVE
To enable women to maintain a strong, loving, passionate relationships in spite of obstacles

LEADER PREPARATION
1. Complete *New Passion for Old Marriages*, chapter six.
2. Compile your own list of the top five or ten disagreements that affect couples' sex lives.
3. Be ready to talk about how you or someone you know cooperated with God to get through a rough time in marriage.
4. Compile a list of resources for women with marital problems by consulting your pastor, leaders in large local churches, as well as your local mental health agencies.
5. Find an appropriate definition of *belong* in the dictionary.

GROUP TIME
1. Compile a list of the top five or ten disagreements that could affect a couple's sex life.
2. Read Song of Solomon 5:1–6:3. What problem between Beloved and Lover does 5:2-6 portray? What role do you think Solomon's obligations as king played in this problem?
3. Dramatize Song 5:2-6, with one volunteer reading Beloved's words in 2:5-6 and a second reading Lover's words.
4. How would you defend Beloved's position? How would you defend Solomon?
5. Scan 1 Corinthians 12:4-31. From this passage, list as many

reasons as time permits for why we should get help from mature trained Christians if marital differences can't be resolved.

6. Look again at Song 5:6, What words here express Beloved's deep feelings?
7. What words could you use to express how you felt at a low point in your marriage?
8. In what ways did God help at that time? What did you have to do to help yourself?
9. Brainstorm a list of resources in your area for couples with marital problems.
10. What experience in your own marriage might enable you to help someone with a troubled marriage?
11. Use readers to perform the following exercise:

   ❦ Reader I: Read aloud Song of Solomon 5:9.
   ❦ Reader II: What's so great about your husband?
   ❦ Reader III: Narrative section for Thursday (pages 64–65).
   ❦ Reader IV: Paraphrase Beloved's answers in Song 5:10-16.

12. What's so great about *your* husband?
13. Read aloud Philippians 4:8. What are some practical ways that you could live it out in your marriage?
14. Read aloud Song of Solomon 6:1-3. Why is verse 3 one of the most important verses in this chapter?
15. Define *belong* as it applies to marriage.
16. In your continuing magazine article titled, "What Every Woman Ought to Know about Marital Intimacy," what all would you include about handling problems that interfere with sexual relations.
17. Pray together for women in your group and others who need help.

JUST YOU AND YOU

❦

LOVING FOR LIFE

OBJECTIVE

To learn ways to remain love partners throughout the stages of one's marriage

LEADER PREPARATION

1. Complete *Loving for Life*, chapter seven.
2. Sort through your memories for a romantic and inexpensive trip you and your husband enjoyed together.
3. Make a note of "waters" that have severely dampened your marriage or the marriage of someone you know. Consider ways through those waters.
4. Create a personal refrain based on Song of Solomon 2:16, 6:3, and 7:10.

GROUP TIME

1. Love between husband and wife must be guarded and protected, nurtured and nourished if it is going to remain strong for life. What pointers have you gleaned thus far from the Song of Solomon that are appropriate for marriage at any stage—from newlywed to golden anniversary?
2. Read aloud Song of Solomon 6:4–8:14. Look more carefully at 6:4, 8-9, and 7:8. What contemporary statements, based on Lover's words to Beloved, could a woman make to her husband?
3. What should a wife do if she isn't honestly able to make one of these statements?
4. Talk about one of the most romantic but inexpensive trips you

have taken with your husband? Why was the trip so successful?

5. Have you ever thought that it's a husband's job to plan romantic interludes? What new perspective do you get from Song 1:4, 7:11-13, and 8:14?

6. Make a list together of Beloved's body parts that Solomon complimented in 6:4-9 and 7:1-7. What habits could you form that might lead you to hear similar praise about these attributes from your own husband as you grow older?

7. Take turns reading aloud Song of Solomon 7:7-9 with someone near you. Do you agree or disagree that passing years don't necessarily make us able to feel comfortable with words like these?

8. How can we cultivate the kind of communication skills the biblical couple had?

9. What do you think most helped Solomon and Beloved make it through their problems? (See Song 1:5-6; 2:15; 5:2-7.)

10. Read Song 8:7. What "waters" or "rivers" have severely dampened your own marital relationship? How did you made it through?

11. The refrain, or phrase repeated in this poem, is found in Song 2:16, 6:3, and 7:10. Brainstorm a refrain based on those thoughts that you could repeat for your own marriage?

12. Consult 1 Corinthians 13:4-7 for specific ways that your husband might like you to demonstrate love to him.

13. What recommendations would you make on how to maintain a loving, sexually enjoyable relationship throughout the years. Include three ideas in your ongoing saga of "What Every Woman Ought to Know about Marital Intimacy."

14. Pray together for wisdom and insight to apply these truths.

Group Guide 8

JUST YOU AND YOU

THE SONG AS ALLEGORY

OBJECTIVE

To see Solomon's poem as allegory and the ways, as such, that it can enrich our lives

LEADER PREPARATION

1. Complete *Intimacy as Allegory*, chapter eight.
2. Think of a time when you've felt separated from God—how and why you came back.
3. Prepare copies of the words to "Jesus, Lover of My Soul".
4. Think of a negative habit or attitude Christ has helped you overcome and popular praise songs that express how that victory makes you feel.
5. Think of three ways to remain enthusiastic about the return of Christ and ways husband and wife can encourage one another in that enthusiasm.

GROUP TIME

1. Look through Song of Solomon, Chapter 2. What words describe Beloved's attitude as she anticipated marriage?
2. What preparations do we need to be making now to become a bride of Christ? See Luke 12:35-48. (Consider regular prayer and Bible study, relationships with family, attitudes toward work and relationships with other believers.)
3. According to Revelation 19:7-8, what will you wear to your wedding to Christ?
4. Why is it possible to have these garments? What thoughts of

gratitude does this bring to your mind?

5. Read aloud Song 2:16, 6:3, and 7:10. Compose a sentence to sum up their main thought.
6. To describe your love for Christ, play the children's game, "I love my love with an A because He is so awesome; I love my love with a B because He is so blessed; etc." Take turns. Help each other come up with words.
7. Sing the hymn, "Jesus, Lover of My Soul."
8. When have you "flown to Christ's bosom" in a tough time? How did you fly to Christ and what were the results?
9. As the king's wife, what were some things Beloved could expect him to do for her?
10. What similar care can we expect from Jesus, our King?
11. What limitations did Solomon have that our King does not?
12. Read the checklists for kingdom members you created on Friday's question three (page 91).
13. Come up with three ways to help yourself anticipate Christ's return.
14. How can a husband and wife help one another anticipate Christ?
15. In your ongoing article, "What Every Woman Needs to Know about Marital Intimacy," what would you include about the Song of Solomon as allegory?
16. Pray sentence prayers based on Revelation 22:20b: "Come, Lord Jesus."

ENDNOTES

Chapter 1

1. J. Vernon McGee, *Through the Bible with J. Vernon McGee*, vol. III, (Pasadena: Through the Bible Radio, 1982), 143.
2. Herbert Lockyer, Sr., general editor, *Nelson's Illustrated Bible Dictionary* (Nashville: Thomas Nelson Publishers, 1986), 1002.
3. Ibid.

Chapter 2

1. Michael G. Maudlin, "Interview with Michael Medved" *Christianity Today* (8 March 1993): 23.
2. Randy C. Alcorn, *Christians in the Wake of the Sexual Revolution* (Portland: Multnomah Press, 1985), 178.

Chapter 4

1. Quentin Crisp, "Sex, Sex, Sex," *Northwest San Francisco Chronicle* (6 May 1990): 8.
2. John F. Walvoord and Roy B. Zuck, *The Bible Knowledge Commentary, Old Testament* (Wheaton, Il.: Victor Books, 1985), 1015
3. Lockyer, *Nelson's Illustrated Bible Dictionary*, 205.
4. David B. Guralink, editor in chief, *Webster's New World Dictionary, Second College Edition* (New York: Prentice Hall Press, 1984), 734.

Chapter 5

1. Joseph C. Dillow, *Solomon on Sex* (Nashville: Thomas Nelson Publishers, 1977), 67.
2. *Lockyer, Nelson's Illustrated Bible Dictionary*, 713.
3. Dillow, *Solomon on Sex*, 74.
4. Guralink, *Webster's New World Dictionary*, 1297.

Chapter 6

1. Lockyer, *Nelson's Illustrated Bible Dictionary*, 713.
2. Dillow, *Solomon on Sex*, 113.

Chapter 7

1. Walvoord and Zuck, *The Bible Knowledge Commentary, Old Testament*, 1022.

Chapter 8

1. Rev. A.R. Fausset, A.M., *A Commentary, Critical, Experimental, and Practical, of the Old and New Testaments* (London: William Collins, Sons, and Company, 1866), xviii.
2. Ibid.
3. Guralink, *Webster's New World Dictionary*, 838.
4. Charles Wesley and Joseph P. Holbrook, *The Chancel Choir* compiled by Cliff Barrows (Philadelphia: Walfred Publishing Co., 1957), 55.

THE TAPESTRY COLLECTION

Michelle Booth
Gold in the Ashes
Eight Studies on Wisdom from Job

Marion Duckworth
Pure Passion
Eight Studies on the Song of Solomon

Marion Duckworth
Renewed on the Run
Nine Studies on 1 Peter

Lin Johnson
Prayer Patterns
Ten Prayers to Weave the Fabric of Your Life

Vicki Lake
Restored in the Ruins
Eight Studies on Nehemiah

Ellen E. Larson and David V. Esterline
More than a Story
Nine Studies on the Parables of Jesus

RuthAnn Ridley
Every Marriage Is Different
Eight Studies on Key Biblical Marriages

Beth Donigan Seversen
Mirror Images
Eight Studies from Colossians